New World Secrets on Ancient Asian Maps

Charlotte Harris Rees

Torchflame Books

Copyright © 2011, 2014 by Charlotte Harris Rees

New World Secrets on Ancient Asian Maps

Charlotte Harris Rees

www.AsiaticFathers.com

harrismaps@msn.com

Published 2014 by Torchflame Books

www.torchflame.com

Durham, NC 27713

Printed in the United States of America

Paperback ISBN: 978-1-61153-110-7

Ebook ISBN: 978-1-61153-109-1

This book is an expansion of *Chinese Sailed to America Before Columbus: More Secrets from the Dr. Hendon M. Harris, Jr. Map Collection*, published 2011 by Authorhouse.

This book is dedicated to the memory of my daughter, Minty, who was part Native American.

Beautiful memories of her burn brightly in my heart.

I grieve now, but look forward to our eternal reunion.

Acknowledgments

I thank the many people who have helped me in the completion of this book. They include my husband Dave Rees and my son Daniel Rees who both spent considerable time helping me. Dr. Cyclone Covey and Dr. Hwa-Wei Lee endorsed this book and have both been a huge encouragement to me. I also thank Kwang On Yoo and Young Ki Lee who both spent many hours studying the information on the maps and Dr. Xiaocong Li and Dr. Gari Ledyard who came to view them. My web master Stuart Whitaker was endlessly patient as was my editor, Jane Lael.

I appreciate the help given to me by Sulia Chan, my brother Hendon Harris, my sister Aurora Harris, Ron Merkle, Fumiko Langley, Randy Beaty, Philip Mulholland, Lam Yee Din, Dr. Edward Lin, Wally Turnbull, Elizabeth Turnbull, and Crofton Held. The Bedford County (Virginia) library staff assisted me in securing many books and articles by inter-library loan.

Several of the photos in this book were taken by Dave Rees. The photos of the *Harris Map Collection* in the CD available through my web site are owned by me but were taken by professional photographer Micah Carroll.

Contents

Introduction

Like someone suddenly awakened in the night in an unfamiliar setting and trying to gain perspective, I stared wide-eyed at the world map. That day in 2003 was the first time I ever saw or touched any of these documents. My family had owned this map collection for decades, but because of their age and fragile condition had decided to handle them only when absolutely necessary. Sketches I had seen did not compare to viewing them in person. Their antiquity made my heart race, as did the unique ways they unfolded from their individual books.

As I gazed, I realized the map I had opened was primitive, and nothing looked familiar. My eyes were drawn to the center. There was what looked to me like the profiled head of a court jester. His mouth gaped. His eye was red, and a red ball hung from the front of his hat. His head was surrounded by a circle of blue, then another squared circle enclosed by yet another circle of blue. I knew that my father saw the right side of the map as the Americas, but I could not get my bearings. How did my father see this as a world map? How could I understand it?

On that date in early 2003 my brother, Hendon Harris, III, a California investor, had flown the maps cross-country so that we and our spouses could take them to the Library of Congress in an attempt to get answers. For decades, since Father's death in 1981, Hendon had kept the collection in a box under his bed, none of us comprehending its real value.

Our father, Dr. Hendon M. Harris, Jr., a third generation Baptist missionary, born in China and fluent in both spoken and written Chinese, found the first of his seven map books in an antique shop in Korea.

Father wrote:

> In August of 1972 I found it necessary to pass through Seoul, Korea. Rising in the morning, I thought that I would use my time by visiting antique shops. In a swift reconnaissance mission I swept through about twenty-five establishments and was about to return to my hotel . . . when I entered one last place. I asked the proprietor if he had any books or pictures. He replied: "Would you be interested in a book of old maps?"

> When I opened the book I noticed it contained many ancient cartographic sketches. There was also a very strange-looking map of Japan that must have

been made at an extraordinarily early date. And then... I opened the last map... and had to control myself to keep from trembling. It was very old and unusual. "Everything Under Heaven" was the title. It was terribly odd. China and Korea took up the center of the world. North of Japan Asia arched round to Alaska. Down the North American coast it was marked "Fu Sang."

I became weak. I was forced to sit down.

Like a sailor suddenly drawn into a whirlpool, Father instantly entered a fray from which he never exited. He spent the rest of his life researching this style of world map and the possibility of the early arrival of Chinese to America.

Publishing an almost 800-page *The Asiatic Fathers of America,* containing two books in one volume, he sought to prove that the Chinese had sailed to the Americas at least 3,500 years before Columbus. When his book came out in the 1970s, it was not widely read. We, his seven children, were skeptical and were too busy with our own lives to join his passionate quest.

The first time he saw the atlas, Father knew it was in Chinese and that the title, *Tian Xia,* on the world map, signified "Everything under Heaven" (the whole earth). Most important to him, that map showed the legendary "Fu Sang" on the American coastline.

Since China's first dynasty, the Xia (start date about 2000 BC), numerous Chinese texts mentioned Fu Sang, "the beautiful land to the East," but no one knew for certain where Fu Sang was. In recent times, many assumed it to be fantasy. However, written three times on the far right side of this map are the words "Fu Sang." Furthermore, most of the place names are countries named in the ancient Chinese geography the *Shan Hai Jing (Classic of Mountains and Seas)*—reportedly written 4,000 years ago and claimed to be surveys to the "ends of the earth."

A map reportedly accompanied the *Shan Hai Jing.*

Father was familiar with Asian classics. He was well aware that the *Shan Hai Jing* was quoted in other Chinese texts, even before the time of Christ and throughout China's exceptionally long history. "Jing" signified that this was a revered classic. Over the centuries, Chinese scholars seeking civil service positions were tested on its contents.

A map reportedly accompanied the *Shan Hai Jing,* but at some unknown time it was separated from the written text. While sitting in the antique store in Seoul in 1972, my father's mind raced. "Was this document a descendant of that long-lost map—copied and re-copied through millennia?"

In January 1981, at only age 64, Father died suddenly of a stroke. We siblings divided his few belongings except for the maps, which we decided to keep together—just in case they proved as earth shattering as our father thought.

However, one year passed into another and they became forgotten documents gathering dust under a bed. Then, in January 2003, I began to wonder whether my father might have been right after all. Shortly thereafter I convinced my brother Hendon to meet me in Washington with the maps.

Hendon and I then took the maps to the Library of Congress where they remained for three years while they were studied. Thinking that this would be a riddle easily and quickly solved, I jumped in with zeal—reading everything I could find on the subject. I was pleasantly surprised to find that my father's obscure book, with a print run of only about 1,000, quoted in several other texts. Years later, I now have read hundreds of books and articles—and I am still reading.

In 2006, I published my edited and abridged version of Father's *The Asiatic Fathers of America: Chinese Discovery and Colonization of Ancient America.* In 2008, I released my own *Secret Maps of the Ancient World,* which brings together much recent research regarding the capability of and evidence for Chinese crossing the Pacific starting in 2000 BC. Then *Chinese Sailed to America Before Columbus: More Secrets from the Dr. Hendon M. Harris, Jr. Map Collection* came out in 2011 and *Did Ancient Chinese Explore America? My Journey Through the Rocky Mountains to Find Answers* in 2013. The book you are reading is derived from and expands *Chinese Sailed to America Before Columbus,* which is now out of print."

The *Harris Maps* have drawn international attention.

The *Harris Map Collection* has drawn considerable international attention. The maps have been discussed on television and radio, and numerous international news articles on them have been published in various languages. Photos of two have been exhibited in museums in Beijing and Australia.

I have been privileged to deliver speeches concerning the maps at the Library of Congress in the United States and the National Library of China in Beijing. I have spoken at numerous venues, including civic organizations, schools, and Tsinghua University in Beijing, the University of Maryland, Stanford University, The University of London, the University of British Columbia, and Simon Fraser University in Canada. In a recent 3 year period, visitors from 147 countries visited my website, *www.AsiaticFathers.com.*

The purpose of this book is to discuss the styles of maps found in the Harris collection and then to give specific information found on the *Harris Maps*—including ancient love notes, state secrets, and internationally volatile data. One geoscientist states that there is information on these maps that has current implications concerning global warming. Most important to historians, these atlases contain information that suggests pre-Columbian Asian contact by sea with the Americas.

A CD containing beautiful professional photos in color of the *Harris Map Collection* is available through *www.AsiaticFathers.com*. With the release of this CD, photos of the entire collection are being shown publicly for the first time.

Chapter 1
Start in the Beginning

"Let's start in the very beginning, a very good place to start."
Lyrics from *The Sound of Music*

I started a study of the meaning of my father's maps as a novice. I now see this as a blessing, not a curse as I initially felt. Hundreds of studies regarding the early arrival of Asians to the Americas have been written, most so academic that the average person has a hard time comprehending them. I slogged through many hours as I read and re-read, doing my best to understand. Though I was deeply interested, the presentation of the material occasionally put me to sleep.

In this book, therefore, I attempt to start the story in the beginning and to tell it simply. However, parts of the story get complex because I have included many quotations from experts on this subject. If those quotations become too cumbersome for your taste, then just skip over them.

If you read *Secret Maps of the Ancient World* first, you will find the concepts in *Chinese Sailed to America Before Columbus* much easier to grasp. *Secret Maps of the Ancient World* explains numerous evidences for the early arrival of Chinese to the Americas by sea. The bibliography to that book lists over 200 texts that you can use as references to start your own research.

Early in my search for validation of the *Harris Maps* and my father's theories concerning them, I discovered several books whose authors mentioned my father. *Dragon Treasures*, written in 1978, quoted heavily from my father and also contained a chapter by Cyclone Covey (PhD, Stanford 1949), who for many decades also did research on the early arrival of Chinese to the Americas.

Via the Internet I located Dr. Covey and asked had he ever heard of my father. (I learned that Covey had quoted Father in four of his books.) Then I asked outright if what Father believed had been disproved by new scientific information.

"Oh, no," Dr. Covey replied. "There is so much more new evidence."

Little knowing what I would confront, I told him that I wanted to reopen Father's research. Dr. Covey offered to assist, and thus became my research mentor.

At first I had to consult Dr. Covey often. He sent me his *A Critical Reprise of "Aboriginal" American History* and suggested other books to read. After I read each set, he kept suggesting more. He was endlessly patient in telling me how to pronounce obscure words or in taking me back to where I could understand. Then we would advance from there. Dr. Covey did his best to not be exasperated with me, but occasionally, while we were on the phone, I heard a quiet sigh.

He became like a father and addressed letters to me as "My very dear Charlotte." I frequently inquired about the health of his lovely wife, Bonnie, and he would proudly say, "She is youthful, as always."

Once when I called Dr. Covey, I discovered he had fallen about five minutes earlier. His wife was trying to convince him that they needed to call the rescue squad. I told him that it might be a stroke and that he needed to call for medical assistance.

"If it is a stroke, it won't do any good to call," he gruffly replied. "There is nothing they can do."

Suddenly *I* was the teacher and yelled into the phone, "Yes they can help you! There are new advancements in medicine. Now hang up the phone and call 911 right now!"

Ten minutes later I sheepishly called back. The rescue people were there. He had experienced a stroke. Dr. Covey had trouble walking for a while, but a few months later he was fine. Throughout the ordeal his mind stayed vibrant. I had prayed for his recovery. Not only did I care for him as an individual, I also desperately needed his help in my quest.

Almost all of my consultations with Dr. Covey have been by phone. In several of our early conversations, though he was speaking English (my native language), he spoke words I did not know. While my vocabulary is better than average, I often flipped through the dictionary to keep up with him.

At one point I joked that he was "Professor Higgins" and I "Eliza Doolittle" from *My Fair Lady*. At times I felt like a grade school student in a post-doctoral course. From the beginning, however, I kept good notes and organized files.

Often each of the different scholars, who wrote the studies I read, believed that *he* had the one definitive answer that would prove the early arrival of Chinese to the Americas by sea. Few individual studies gained much attention. However, it forms a tsunami of compelling evidence when one brings their research together in one book, as was done in *Secret Maps of the Ancient World*.

While there is a great deal of proof now, many researchers have not communicated their findings in language that can be understood by the masses. From the mindset of one who originally knew nothing about these maps and this subject, I here share what I have learned.

The basic premises for this book:

1. **My father's maps are in Korean atlases.**

2. **The primitive world maps in these atlases show Fu Sang on the American coastline.** They are written in Chinese characters and seventy-two percent of the place names are from the *Shan Hai Jing*[1]—a Chinese geography written around 2000 BC. **Therefore, my father and others believed that his maps, though in Korean atlases, had descended from earlier Chinese maps.**

3. **Since we are discussing the Chinese, I attempt to stay within a historical timeline of China.** From 1995 to 2000, hundreds of Chinese academics from numerous disciplines conducted an exhaustive study that concluded that China's first dynasty, the Xia, started about 2070 BC and that the culture was far more advanced than previously thought.[2] There is evidence that the Chinese were oceangoing, had a written language, and were making silk at that time. Therefore, I do not go back earlier, and for simplicity I use 2000 BC as a starting date.

4. **There are unexplained indicators of advanced civilizations appearing suddenly in the Americas starting around 2000 BC as well as items from the Americas found in Asia dating to the same time period.** Numerous examples[3] include banana leaves and old world cotton found in the Americas, and American peanuts found in more than one Chinese site. Because those advanced civilizations appeared in South America before they appeared in North America implies sea travel. DNA studies suggest the same thing. (See *Secret Maps of the Ancient World* for more detail.)

5. **Writings attributed to China's first dynasty and quoted throughout Chinese history claim travels to the ends of the earth.** Other ancient Chinese writings indicate knowledge of the Americas. One Chinese writer in the third century BC stated that Fu Sang was 10,000 li (3,300 miles) wide—almost the exact width of North America—and had enormous trees. How could someone in China that long ago have known this unless someone had been to the Americas?

6. **Even with simple boats, distant travel was possible using prevailing ocean currents.** From at least the Warring States period, 403-221 BC, and onward, Chinese wrote about one eastward flowing current that they named "*Wei Lu.*"[4] In the 20th century, several groups demonstrated that they could cross the Pacific on rafts or very small boats floating on these very same currents.[5]

    The US National Oceanic and Atmospheric Administration (NOAA) states that the main current in the North Pacific is warm and is 100 kilometers (62 miles) wide and one kilometer (.6 mile) deep at maximum depth. In volume it is equivalent to 6,000 Danube Rivers.[6] That current, a conveyor shaped like a giant racetrack, continuously brings objects from Asia to North America and then back.[7]

In *Chinese Maritime Activities and Socioeconomic Development, 2100 B.C.-1900 A.D.,* my friend Dr. Gang (Kent) Deng of the London School of Economics explains early Chinese sea capabilities. Notice how early he has Chinese at sea.

7. **During most of world history, China was the most advanced society on earth.** Several European and American researchers have confirmed this. According to Joseph Needham of Cambridge University, numerous inventions credited to Europeans actually were invented in China and were in use there hundreds of years prior.

8. **Early Chinese writings describe the Americas.** Some of the descriptions are very precise, stating "go so many *li* and you will see" such and such. (A Chinese li is approximately 1/3 mile.) These very specific geographic details fit no place on earth other than the Americas. Several of these written journeys have been charted onto maps of America.[8]

9. **In all of history there have been increases in, then losses of knowledge.** Sometimes, in both East and West, information was lost during times of war or political upheaval. Also, consider the Dark Ages in Europe. Around the time Europe was coming out of the Dark Ages, China shut down to the outside world—and retreated into a period when much knowledge was lost.

10. **To understand maps of any part of the world one needs a basic understanding of the history of that area.** Most American schools teach little about Asian history. We can compensate for this deficit by reading and independent study.

Because we never heard of something before does not make it false.

---

11. **The more we learn, the more we realize that there are additional concepts to grasp about the world in which we live.** We need to weigh all the evidence with an open mind. Because someone wrote on a subject does not make what he or she wrote true. On the other hand, because we never heard of something before does not make it false, either. There are many interesting "rabbit trails" in this study, and one has to constantly bring oneself back to focus.

12. *Tian Xia* **is the Chinese name and** *Ch'onhado* **the Korean name for the style of world map found in these atlases.** My father referred to his world map as the *Harris Fu Sang Map.* However, as it depicts much more than just Fu Sang, I call it the *Harris World Map.* My references to *Harris Maps* or the *Harris Map Collection* include all the different maps in the seven atlases my father owned.

Chapter 2

Setting the Stage

In college, though I was a good student, my least favorite subject was history. I took those classes only because they were required for graduation. I hated memorizing dates and information about "dead people." History was as dry as old bones. My interest then was in understanding myself, my peers, and the here and now.

Now, however, I find history alive and breathing, telling a story that is straightforward, yet more complicated than any of us can fully comprehend.

History is as simple as a story of the lives of real people who felt all the emotions we feel today—love, pride, joy, grief, fear, anger, and sorrow. These lines from "In Flanders Field," penned by Lieutenant Colonel John McCrae of the Canadian Army during World War I, say it well:

> We are the dead. Short days ago we lived, felt dawn, saw sunset glow, loved and were loved, and now we lie in Flanders field.[1]

Whenever I forget emotions and individual lives, history reverts to cold, hard facts.

Throughout history, the beauty of sunsets and rainbows awed most people. Some lives were ordinary, some heroic, others tragic. DNA shows that the genetic code of all people is 99.9 percent the same.[2] Emotionally, people are similar around the world. Sometimes the difference is just how and when those emotions are expressed. Whenever I forget emotions and individual lives, history again reverts to cold, hard facts.

One of the *Harris Maps* has love notes written in its ancient folds. Who were the lovers? Did the lover return from his trip or was the map brought back without him? Did they feel pride in their children and grief at the loss of a loved one? Did they enjoy watching sunsets and rainbows into their old age?

Some of the *Harris Maps* contain state secrets, including instructions for where a country's citizens should hide in time of war. If information on that map about where to hide was ever used, was the official fearful while he disseminated it? Did sweat rise on his brow? How did young mothers with babies feel when they had to flee?

One of the *Harris Maps* contains information that is now at the center of an international dispute about who owns a particular island[3] and rights to the gas hydrates in that region. Little did the mapmaker know that by including that tiny rocky island on his map that his documentation could protect rights to enough fuel to satisfy the modern Korean demand for thirty years?[4] That might be the most significant contribution of that mapmaker's entire life.

The maps themselves are printed on fine mulberry bark paper, produced in a laborious process undertaken in water during the winter months. My fingers ache with cold when I visualize that.

World history is complicated as it spans millennia, and people and nations acted and reacted in many different ways. To understand what took place, it helps to know the timeline and to know what else was happening in the world that precipitated those actions and responses— just as when a parent asks who did what first when the offspring get into an argument.

Though we believe that the *Tian Xia,* the distinctive round world map, originated in an earlier time, the *Harris Maps* and others like them circulated during the Joseon Dynasty of Korea. The Joseon Dynasty (sometimes referred to as Choson, Chosun, or Yi) lasted from AD 1392 to 1910. In this book I discuss the three main actors on the stage of Asia during that era— China, Japan, and Korea.

During this same period, Europe experienced rapid scientific and technological development. European nations started voyages of exploration that stretched all the way to Asia. The explorers were accompanied or soon followed by individuals on commercial and/or religious quests.

China

As a main character in this study, I consider China the larger big brother.

As stated earlier, Chinese history goes back to the 21st century BC and spans over 4,000 years. It has been established that by the time of their first dynasty, the Xia, the Chinese civilization was advanced. Its people sailed the oceans, had a written language, and were making silk. According to Barnes and Noble's *Timechart History of the World,* 2000 BC was not long after the founding of Egypt and Greece and was roughly the time of Abraham of the Old Testament.[5]

For millennia, Chinese civilization was the most advanced on earth. However, as stated earlier, in any society there are times of knowledge gained and knowledge lost. Perhaps the largest loss for China started in the early 15th century when Chinese leaders chose to shut their country off from the rest of the world for several hundred years.

Needham wrote the many volumes of *Science and Civilisation in China*, which some claim is one of the greatest works of scholarship undertaken by a single person in the 20th century. Robert Temple wrote *The Genius of China: 3,000 Years of Science, Discovery, and Invention,* in which he reduced Needham's work into one book in layman's language.

For millennia, Chinese civilization was the most advanced on earth.

These two men demonstrate that the early Chinese were extremely innovative. In the 14th century BC the Chinese had a decimal system (2,300 years before the West). In the 13th century BC they had the first plastic (lacquer) (3,200 years before the West). In the sixth century BC Chinese had iron plows (2,200 years before the West) and understood circulation of the blood (1,800 years before the West). In the fifth century BC they conducted geo-biological prospecting (2,100 years before the West). In the fourth century BC Chinese wrote about the first law of motion (2,000 years before Newton), used petroleum and natural gas as fuel (1,400 years before the West), and had manned flight with kites (1,650 years before the West.)[6] These are but a few of China's early discoveries and inventions.

For most of China's history there was an elite class of intellectuals, and the emperors ruled a slave state. Though there were innovations, they were not necessarily used in all of China.

The famous Chinese Admiral Zheng He, who made many voyages between AD 1405 and 1433, claimed to have sailed more than 100,000 li (33,000 miles) of the world's oceans and seas.[7]

Richard Smith, Professor of Humanities at Rice University, wrote in *Chinese Maps: "Images of All Under Heaven"*: "The termination of Zheng's expeditions in 1433 provoked by the powerful opposition of Confucian scholars to 'wasteful' maritime adventures signaled a precipitous decline in Chinese interest in people overseas."[8]

This decision dramatically changed world history. By then, many of Zheng He's crew and numerous privately owned ships had been at sea for years. In 1433, China shut down to the outside world, other than to a few close neighbors such as Korea, which China later also forced into isolation.

The Portuguese reached China in 1514, followed by the Spanish, Dutch, and British through the 1700s. The United States and other European countries arrived in the 1800s.[9]

Matteo Ricci and other Catholic missionaries went to China in the 16th century. Their influence was felt in the collaborative world map and in other maps of China that followed. However, theological debate between the different groups of Catholics and later the Protestants caused the Chinese to distrust them. Growing hostility in China to the Western missionaries resulted in a 1724 ban of Christianity by the emperor,[10] a ban later rescinded.

Smith wrote: "During the late eighteenth and early nineteenth centuries, Westerners came to China in ever-greater numbers, driven quite literally by the powerful engines of the Industrial Revolution. Merchants pursued commercial gain, while missionaries sought converts."[11] More and more Westerners arrived. Some were not willing to just be visitors and attempted (sometimes successfully) to influence politics.

For most of its history, China was self-ruled, but from 1264 to 1368, China was ruled by the Mongols, and from 1644 to 1911 by the Manchus.[12]

Korea

As another main character in this study, Korea took the role of the younger brother.

Sometimes China was an ally of Korea. However, at various times through this era China forced his will on Korea. In this way Korea was compelled by his stronger sibling (China) to do one thing or another. Sometimes Korea fought back. Other times Korea submitted. Every time Korea would have preferred to make his own decisions.

Like the Chinese culture, Korean cultures also go back to similar early times. Starting between 108 and 313 BC, 100 Chinese colonies were established across Korea and among its varied cultures.[13]

Harris wrote:

> The Koreans were the first foreign people with whom the Japanese had relationships. Klaproth [an 18th century German scholar who devoted his life to Asian studies] says that there was constant communication between China and Korea, and that Korea paid tribute to China throughout the fifth and sixth centuries.
>
> When the Chinese visited Japan it was normally by way of Korea. . . . the Chinese relied upon the Koreans for information as to the route to Japan, and for assistance in reaching that country; and that . . . assistance of the Koreans was a vital element in the journey of the Five Monks [AD fifth century] to America. . . . without the Koreans the trip itself could not have been made. In our own researches we would never have been inspired to do what we have done unless we had Korean information. We understand that at the time of one great book burning, a Korean scholar preserved many priceless manuscripts, maps, etc. by adding false walls to the interior of his house and concealing the priceless manuscripts . . . between the walls. Furthermore it is generally accepted that Asia has no scholars more meticulous in their work than the Koreans.[14]

Through a coup in 1392, the Yi family had taken control of Korea. Therefore, the Joseon period is also known as the Yi Dynasty. Those who dominated Korean politics of that era were called the "meritorious elite." They were granted slaves and large agricultural tracts to be held in perpetuity.[15] They were the scholars—and limited education almost exclusively to their own.[16] Meanwhile, the peasants were heavily taxed and conscripted for military service. Unable to meet their obligations, many of the poor abandoned their land and became wanderers.

Bae Woo Sung (PhD in Korean history, Seoul National University) stated in the Spring 2008 *Korea Journal* published by the Korean National Commission for UNESCO:

> By the time of Joseon's foundation, the Ming [Chinese] dynasty was the dominant power on the Asian continent. Ming employed an inward-looking foreign policy, and Ming rulers prohibited their subjects from having free maritime contact with foreigners. As far as the opportunity for official contact with the external world was concerned, the international setting of Joseon was less favorable than that of Goryeo [the Korean dynasty pre-1392].[17]

Furthermore, Korea was steeped in neo-Confucianism, which encouraged development of the inner mind before exploration. Koreans of that era had neither ability nor much desire for world travel. This was one of the least likely times for a world map to emerge from Korea.

As in any sibling relationship, the younger brother often took on the habits and customs of the older brother. However, when Koreans adopted something from China, they frequently improved on it.

Chinese invented paper in the second century BC.[18] The earliest paper was made from hemp or mulberry tree bark.[19] Koreans perfected it to the point that some Chinese preferred Korean paper, and it became famous across Asia. A renowned Chinese poet of the 11th century asked to publish his anthology on fine paper imported from Korea.

Mulberry bark paper, such as that on which the *Harris Maps* are printed, was made in a complicated and laborious process by skilled artisans. Manufacturing required numerous steps—all painstakingly done by hand. Part of the process had to be done in water during the cold winter months to keep the product from spoiling. Korea is about as far north as New York. Buildings were poorly heated. Making the mulberry bark paper was so difficult that most artisans in that trade wished a better occupation for their children.

In the West, paper products rarely last even 300 years. Korea has mulberry bark paper books that are almost 1,000 years old. In making this paper, bark from cut branches is stripped into three layers—the black outer, the green middle, and the white inner.

The finest paper is made of white bark only. Any other color fiber is carefully picked out, and sheets are made of many very thin layers. The process is so revered that the Korean government has now "appointed the masters of Korean papermaking as intangible cultural assets and protects the industry with special care"[20] to keep this art from dying.

Printing was invented in China. In the eighth century, Chinese were printing from carved wooden blocks. To prepare a printing block, the part of the text that was to remain white had to be cut away with a knife. This type of printing moved to Korea that same century.

In the 11th century, Chinese had moveable type made of clay.[21] By 1234, the Koreans had moveable type made of metal.[22] However, even after the introduction of moveable type, some things, such as maps, continued to be printed from carved wooden blocks. After many printings, the quality of the print from wooden blocks became less crisp.

"In 1392, King Gongyang [of Korea] gave the government office Seojeokwon (books and publications center) the responsibility of overseeing all matters related to casting metal type and printing books."[23]

Koreans originally used Chinese script exclusively. The Korean system of writing called Han'gul came into being in 1446. Following that date, many books were published in Han'gul. *A New History of Korea* stated: "Nevertheless, the many works of major importance compiled under government auspices continued on the whole to be written in Chinese."[24] The fact that the *Harris Maps* are in Chinese could be proof of their origin and/or their government connection.

Japanese raids of Korea began at early dates. They came by sea again in the 13th century. The raids increased in the mid 14th century to the point that farmers moved inland, letting their coastal lands lie fallow.[25] For a period of time, Korean maritime traffic came to a standstill. Korea tried unsuccessfully to solve this by several diplomatic missions to Japan. To protect themselves, the Koreans built a navy.

In 1592, the Japanese invaded Korea. Ki-baik Lee wrote in *A New History of Korea* that it was at this point that the Korean Naval commander Yi Sun-sin:

> energetically set about building warships and training their crews. In particular, on the model of vessels already in use since the mid-fifteenth century, he built his famed "turtle ships" (kobukson) with a protective covering (thought to have been iron plated) to ward off enemy arrows and shells, and in addition with numerous spikes implanted to prevent the enemy from boarding. He also emplaced cannon around the entire circumference of the ships, so that attack could be made at will from any side. . . . Admiral Yi's successes gave complete control of the sea lanes to the Korean force.[26]

Model replica of the Korean armored turtle ship at
The Maritime Museum, Oxnard, CA. (Photo by Dave Rees)

Meanwhile, battles on land continued. Ming Chinese troops 50,000 strong came to Korea's defense.

Japan attacked again by sea in 1597. Though this was only five years after Yi's brilliant success in 1592, through intrigue Yi had lost his position as naval commander. The Japanese fleet overwhelmingly defeated the new Korean admiral. "The . . . government hastily reinstated Admiral Yi who with the mere dozen warships remaining in his command won a resounding victory."[27]

In the seven-year period from 1592 to 1598, "nearly the whole of Korea's eight provinces became an arena of Japanese pillage and slaughter."[28] There was also a great loss of cultural treasures, and "volumes stored in three of the four History Archives (Sago) were reduced to ashes."[29] During that time, many other books and artifacts were taken from Korea to Japan.

In mid-1598, the Japanese completely withdrew. Korea and Japan entered into a peace treaty in 1606. Ki-baik Lee understated: "the animosity of the Korean people toward Japan remained alive long thereafter."[30] The Manchus from the North invaded Korea in 1627 and 1636.

While the Ming Chinese had been busy in the late 16th century defending Korea, their opponents in Manchuria became more powerful and soon ruled China as the Ch'ing Dynasty.

Korea withdrew into its shell in defense. "After this the Choson government followed a policy of seclusion, restricting its interaction with Japan largely to ceremonial contacts . . . and limiting its contact with China to a few tributary missions a year."[31]

Until the middle of the 19th century Korea rebuffed even the Europeans who tried to enter. Perhaps the last record of turtle ships was when one was used against an American merchant ship, the *General Sherman,* which had tried to force its way into Korea in 1866. Finally, the Japanese, in a staged incident in 1875, forced Korea to open up.[32]

Part of the Korean government's reason for wanting to be isolated was that Western powers seemed to be taking over China and Japan—and they did not want a similar fate. In Korea Catholicism had been spreading rapidly among the poor and oppressed, and the government feared uprisings.

Following the *General Sherman* incident, by some accounts up to 10,000 Korean Christians were brutally murdered by the Korean government in an attempt to protect Korea from Western influence.

The choices in Korea had been either to keep the old, or to get rid of the old and accept the new. During the period of isolation, Korea opted to keep the old and thus kept its old maps.

When in 1884 American Presbyterian missionary Horace N. Allen introduced Protestant Christian beliefs, many Koreans eagerly embraced them.[33] The Christian church is strong in Korea today.

Japan

In this drama, perhaps Japan can be considered the belligerent neighbor of Korea and China rather than a brother.

China, Korea, and Japan are all related genetically, but the relationship between China and Korea at most times was friendlier than that between either of them and Japan.

The distance from Fukuoka, Japan, to Pusan, South Korea, is only 130 miles (210 kilometers). From the outlying islands, the distance is much closer. Frequently the Japanese tried to take what was not theirs. At times China tried to defend Korea from Japan. Most likely that was to keep Korea as a buffer between China and Japan, but nevertheless, China intervened.

Although cultures in that area existed earlier, Japan was first unified around AD 400. About that time, Chinese writing was introduced and there was "an inflow of foreign visitors, new skills and knowledge imported from China and Korea, the introduction of iron farm tools and weapons throughout Japan, and the introduction of Buddhism. By the end of the fourth century, Japan went to war against Korea."[34]

Throughout history, Japan was involved in much bloodshed. The 16th century was marked by civil wars between competing lords, followed by wars against neighboring countries. In the

17th century, shoguns sought peace at all cost, and the 250 years thereafter were relatively tranquil.[35]

Nevertheless, Japan repeatedly took up war against China and/or Korea. One does not need to know either Koreans or Chinese long to hear them complain about Japan.

The latest and perhaps cruelest times were when Japanese occupied Korea from 1910 through 1945 (the end of World War II) and when they occupied parts of China from 1937 through the end of World War II.

Unfathomable atrocities such as biological warfare,[36] the rape of Nanjing and other cities in China, the purposeful slaughter of Christians in Korea—asking them to step forward then shooting them and burning them in their churches[37]—and pilfering of national treasures occurred during that time at the hands of the Japanese.

That most of those crimes were never judged after World War II, as war crimes were in Europe, leave those Asian wounds raw—even today. Koreans report that they lost many of their old maps as a result of the Japanese occupation. This could explain why some of the oldest existing Asian maps are found today in Japan rather than in their native countries.[38]

The only two original copies of Korea's 1402 *Kangnido* map still in existence are both in Japan. Of the only six known complete sets of Ricci's 1602 Chinese world map, three are in Japan and in no other Asian country.[39] Several of Korea's old *Ch'onhado* maps are in Japanese collections. Japanese claim to have these maps simply because they revere old maps.

At the Asian Division of the Library of Congress is a display of documents, including maps, taken by the Allies at the end of World War II from captured Japanese troops—all stolen by the Japanese during their occupation of China.

With the arrival of the Western powers, Japan also had the choice of staying with the old or embracing the new. In contrast to Korea, Japan chose the new. That is reflected in the more modern maps that circulated in Japan during that era.

However, when missionaries tried to introduce Christianity to Japan, most Japanese rejected it. In fact, Japanese hatred for Christianity played out during their occupations of China and Korea when they encountered Christians.

Chapter 3
Mapmaking from an Asian Perspective

Caucasians, such as I, are used to seeing world maps produced by Americans with the Americas in the middle, or those done by Europeans, with Europe in the center and America on the far left. For us it seems odd to view the Americas on the far right because virtually none of the maps we use are drawn that way.

Early Asian world maps had China as the central focus, as do maps of Asia today. This is known as a Sinocentric view. The Chinese name for China literally translates as "middle kingdom," meaning "center of civilization." Some have complained that the Chinese were egotistical to put China in the middle of their maps. However, all travelers begin a journey from wherever they are, so naturally put their own country as the central focus of their maps.

Some point out that on Sinocentric maps China downplayed the size of other countries. China, however, is not alone in self-promotion. An Australian world map turns the world upside down so that the map is oriented to the south and Australia is at the top—the "king of the hill." The 1402 *Kangnido* map inflates Korea to at least one-third the size of China.[1] The *Mercator* world map, currently used in many Western schools and atlases, exaggerates the size of Europe and the Northern hemisphere.

In Eastern Origins of Western Civilization, John Hobson of the University of Sheffield wrote with irony that "the irrelevance of the East and the superiority of Europe is . . . 'confirmed' by the *Mercator* world map . . . the actual landmass of the southern hemisphere is exactly twice that of the northern hemisphere. And yet on the *Mercator,* the landmass of the North occupies two-thirds of the map while the landmass of the South represents only a third."[2] Therefore, how can we honestly single out Chinese for exaggeration?

One may wonder why maps today have north at the top and not south, east, or west. While most of the rest of the world was still using various orientations for their maps, Taoists in Asia, based on religious belief, put north at the top. Perhaps the north orientation that we now use was borrowed from Asia.

For thousands of years, Chinese kept extensive charts of stars, eclipses, and comets. According to Needham: "The oldest record of a nova or supernova in any civilization . . . [is] a Shang [Chinese] oracle-bone [writing] dating from about 1300 BC."[3]

Needham wrote: "Chinese were the most persistent and accurate observers of celestial phenomena in any culture before the Renaissance."[4] Star maps of the night sky were divided into twenty-eight segments. When the rest of the world caught up to China in astronomy, they consulted those early Asian records. By referencing positions of the stars, early travelers by land or sea were able to go far distances and return home safely.

Chinese writings indicate that they were from early dates not only mapping the sky but also the earth. In *History of Cartography,* Leo Bagrow wrote: "Chinese tradition places the first maps in around 2000 B.C."[5] The earliest Chinese maps, dating from 2000 BC, were reportedly on bronze vessels on tripods. Later maps were on rock, bamboo, or silk. In 126 BC, the Chinese emperor looked at maps to see the distant places his ambassador had visited.[6]

Shang Dynasty bronze vessel on tripod

In the second century, Zhang Heng of China invented quantitative cartography. In AD 267, P'ei Hsiu was appointed China's Minister of Works. P'ei wrote: "The origin of maps and geographical treatises goes far back into former ages. Under the three dynasties [Xia, Shang, and Zhou—the first of which started about 2000 BC] there were special officials for this."[7]

Model of Zhang Heng's second century armillary (celestial globe) at Beijing airport.

P'ei explained that none of the maps from those early eras were made using a graduated scale or a rectangular grid, and that their arrangement was imperfect and rough. He devised six principles for making a map:

1. Use graduated division to determine scale.
2. Use a rectangular grid.
3. Pace out sides of right-angled triangles to fix distance.
4. Measure the high and the low.
5. Measure right angles and acute angles.
6. Measure curves and straight lines.[8]

Bagrow wrote: "Maps reached a high point in their development when paper was invented in A.D. 105."[9]

This three foot square *Map of the Tracks of Yu*, found near Xi'an is carved in stone. Created in 1137, it shows the coastline and all the major river systems of China. It is covered by a grid of squares – each 100 li. This is in line with P'ei's system of mapping detailed above. Since Chinese maps were that advanced in 1137, it leads one to believe that if *Tian Xia* maps (like the one shown on the cover of this book) were also from China, they must have originated much earlier.

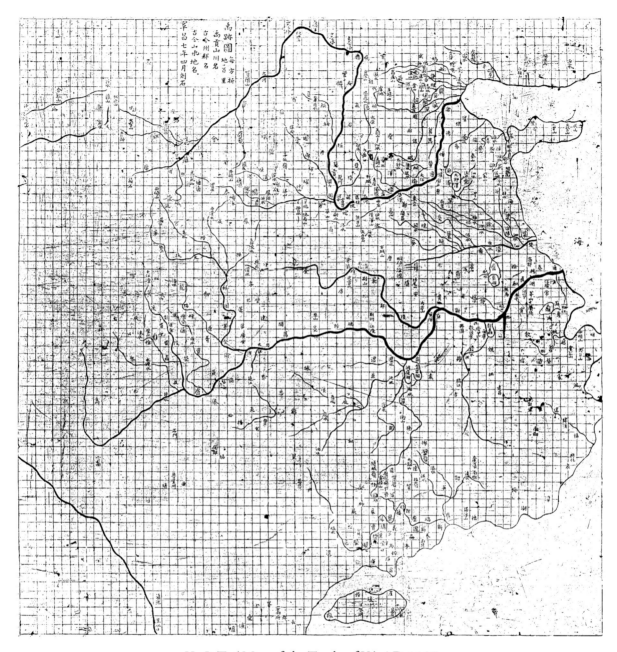

Yu Ji Tu (*Map of the Tracks of Yu*) AD 1137

Dr. Hiroshi Nakamura, an early 20th century Japanese expert on Asian maps, wrote that a traditional story recounts that Marco Polo took an Asian world map back to Italy in 1295,[10] but it is unknown what that map looked like. What Asian world map was even in existence at that time unless it was the *Tian Xia*?

Matteo Ricci's map was introduced to China in 1602 and has many features that show collaboration between Chinese and Western ideas. However, after a few short years, Chinese rejected the Ricci maps in favor of ones influenced by geomancy (tied to feng shui). This is an example of a time when knowledge seemed to be lost.

Richard Smith stated, concerning those geomancy-inspired maps:

> Chinese were not above adding topographical features such as hills or mountains
> to their cartographic productions in order to depict (or create) a more favourable
> geomantic environment.[11] . . . from the late seventeenth century into the early
> nineteenth, the vast majority of Chinese map-makers ignored Jesuit constructions
> of the world almost entirely. . . . None of these works [during that time] show
> the slightest concern with mathematic accuracy.[12]

Following this period of contrived maps, the Sino-Japanese war in the mid-nineteenth century
caused the Chinese to realize that they needed realistic maps.

Korean and Japanese maps were often borrowed from the Chinese.

Koreans and Japanese acknowledge that their maps for hundreds of years were based on Chinese
principles and were often borrowed from Chinese cartography. Shannon McCune (PhD in
geography, born in Korea to Presbyterian missionary parents) stated that "Korean cartography
has had a long and interesting history with close relations to Chinese cartography."[13]

Han Young-woo wrote in *The Artistry of Early Korean Cartography* that a Korean tomb from
the fourth century excavated in 1953 contained a map of a Chinese city.[14] However, maps
were tied to national security and sharing of maps between countries was not always allowed.
In 1148, two Korean officials died in jail after being accused of attempting to send their
privately owned maps of Korea to China.[15]

Bae stated that "a great majority of Joseon maps of the world and foreign countries were
made from imported source maps. . . . Their most important factor seems to have been their
Sinocentric worldview."[16]

Han stated that "Korea started making world and East Asian maps as early as the Koryo
period. Yi Kyubo (1168-1241) . . . wrote an introduction to a map called the *Hwaido (Map
of China and the Barbarians)*. He stated in his introduction that the map included all the
countries in the world including Korea."[17]

In Asia, from the 15th through the 19th centuries, many maps were printed using carved
wooden blocks.[18]

Depictions of the Ricci 1602 map came relatively soon to Korea. A copy of the map reached
Seoul in 1603. Han stated that "The *Tushu bian (Compilation of Illustrations and Writings)* .
. . published by Zhang Huang in 1613 . . . was imported to Korea . . . and read by many. .
. . The *Tushu bian* included a variety of pictures and maps including a world map based on
Matteo Ricci's."[19]

In 1630, a Korean emissary to China brought back *Zhifang Waiji (Notes on World Geography)* written by missionary Giulio Aleni. That text included *Wanguo quantu (Complete Map of the Myriad Countries),* a modern world map.[20] Then, in 1708, a Korean painter hand-copied Ricci's map and brought that copy back to Korea.[21] Therefore, the fact that many Koreans preferred *Ch'onhado* maps through the 19th century was not because they were ignorant of more modern world maps.

Han stated that "the *Nihongi (Chronicles of Japan) . . .* records that a Korean monk named Kwanruk of Paekche brought geography to Japan."[22]

Although maps had been hand drawn in Japan since at least AD 646,[23] a map of T'ang China reprinted in 1494 from the original was reported to be the earliest map printed in Japan.

In the 17th century, the Japanese eagerly accepted the Ricci world map. A derivation of Ricci was printed in 1645 in Japanese phonetic letters (kana).[24] From then on, Japanese world maps modeled after Ricci dominated, including a beautiful 17th century Japanese world map (now at the University of British Columbia) shown online.[25]

Nagakubo Sekisui, a Japanese Confucian scholar of Mito, published an even more modern map in 1785, also in the Matteo Ricci style. Several different variations of the Sekisui map followed.[26] Maps made by the shoguns became quite accurate. They used surveying methods learned from the Chinese.

The Japanese developed an appreciation for maps, but moved away from maps centered on China. However, they still considered Japan, China, and India as the three great world powers.[27]

Many old maps produced in Japan have color added (as it has been on some of the *Harris Maps.*) Nanba Matsutaro, who co-authored *Old Maps in Japan,* stated: "It was common practice to add brilliant colors to maps . . . presented to a shogun or daimyo."[28] Color was added by hand until the late 18th century when multicolored printing developed in Japan. Copperplate printing was also introduced about that same time.[29]

Even the question of why we use the English word "orient" to mean both "the Far East" and "to know one's location" speaks to the fact that Asians were among the first to know their place on the globe. Nevertheless, we all need an Asian perspective to understand an Oriental map.

Chapter 4

The *Tian Xia* (*Ch'onhado*)
"Everything Under Heaven" World Map
Layout Explained

"I set my mind to seek and explore by wisdom
concerning all that has been done under heaven."
Ecclesiastes 1:13

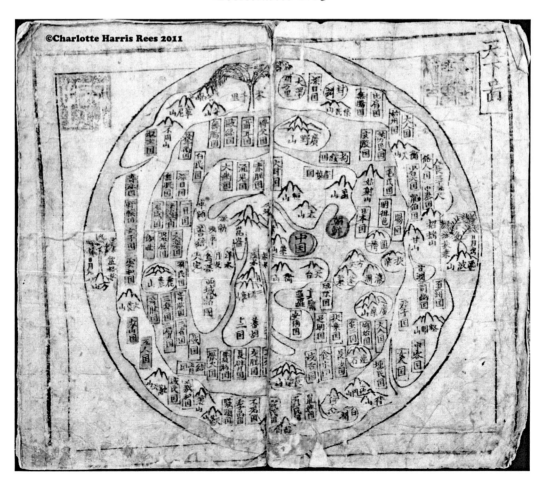

Harris World Map 5

"*Tian Xia,*" the title of this map in Chinese, literally means "everything under heaven" or "the whole earth." *Tian Xia*, however, is more or less a generic title meaning "world map," as is the Korean name for this map, *Ch'onhado.*

Though the map above that my father found in the antique shop in 1972 was the first of its kind that he had ever seen, he soon discovered a few others in collections and famous museums around the world. Sometimes these are found as single maps, but are usually part of an atlas.

Even in 1947, when Dr. Hiroshi Nakamura wrote "Old Chinese Maps Preserved by the Koreans" for the prestigious *Imago Mundi*, he stated, concerning *Tian Xia* map books, that "always they were treated as rare and precious books, not only in Europe but even in Japan where amateurs, collectors, and even libraries considered them as rare."[1]

Dr. Gari Ledyard, Professor Emeritus, Columbia University, pointed out in *The History of Cartography* that an important feature of Korean *Ch'onhado* maps was their position in an atlas. He stated:

> The usual mode of publication was as the first map in an atlas. After one looked at the *world* [emphasis mine], one could turn the page and peruse more detailed maps of the countries that were important because of their proximity . . . [such as] China [or] Japan . . . These were followed by a general map of Korea and individual maps of its individual eight provinces. Many such albums also had tables indicating the location of postal and military stations.[2]

China is the focus of this map, not Korea.

Though many consider this distinct design (style) of map to be Korean because it was found in Korea, the text is always in Chinese and it focuses on China, not Korea. Oh Sang-Hak (Assistant Professor of Geography in Korea) stated in the *Korea Journal* that in many of these maps:

> The name of . . . "China" . . . is significantly framed in a circle, and . . . "Korea" appears in name only without a frame, while other neighboring countries are framed in rectangles . . . . It mirrors the . . . view of China as the central culture and country in the world, with Korea as a "little China" and others as uncivilized barbarians.[3]

Some maps have fewer countries listed, but McCune insisted that "there is a precise limitation to 145 place names."[4] (There are exceptions to every rule. *The History of Cartography* mentions that a few *Ch'onhado* have more countries, which some experts suggest may mean they are more recent maps.)[5]

Lee Chan, author of *Old Maps of Korea* produced by the Korean Library Science Research Institute, argued that:

> The very idea of viewing the world as a circle seems to have come from China, but it was the Koreans who presented the idea in a map . . . . The map was widely disseminated owing to the development of printing techniques. The maps are true to the prototype, but they vary slightly in minute content and shape. This was the favorite world map of that time until modern Western world maps were introduced in Korea.[6]

In the 1990 *The Journal of Modern Korean Studies (Kundae Hanguk yongu)*, Shannon McCune wrote a very insightful article on the *Ch'onhado*. He makes many good points and the eight pages of that article[7] bear reading in their entirety.

McCune stated that hand drawn copies of the *Ch'onhado* were more prevalent than those printed from carved wood blocks. He wrote that there were "at least 13 different editions [of the printed *Ch'onhado*] during the period from roughly 1500 to 1880."[8]

Those printed from carved blocks were "limited editions" since each carved block could print only so many before the print became fuzzy and the block had to be replaced.

Printed *Ch'onhado* maps are the most valuable.

Bagrow stated that maps printed from wooden blocks were more highly prized in the East because they were a luxury compared to those copied by hand.[9] (It was an issue of supply and demand. Anyone could draw this simple map, but there were only a limited number of printed copies.) All of the maps in the *Harris Map Collection* were printed from wooden blocks.

Some manuscript copies now in existence were drawn by students. McCune stated that "the copies drawn by a Korean scholar-cartographer or a skilled copyist have delicate and beautiful calligraphy"[10] and thus were more valuable than those drawn by a student. However, the printed ones were still the most coveted.

Atlases that contain a *Ch'onhado* map often include other maps originally produced at different times. Dating the most recent map or text entry helps one discover when each atlas was assembled. Therefore, information on all maps in each atlas has to be considered.

For instance, in 2004, the Smithsonian displayed a hand drawn *Ch'onhado* found in an atlas. Because of an 1828 census in that atlas, that particular map was determined to have been produced sometime between 1828 and 1884, the date it was purchased by an American sailor.[11]

Most of these *Ch'onhado* maps do not have notes, but some have annotations of astronomical "misinformation" such as the distance between the four poles, or between heaven and earth. My father found it charming that the early mapmakers were doing their best to be helpful.

What Do the Ancient Round Maps Signify?

Before my father's death in 1981, his map collection had grown to seven map books. In *The Asiatic Fathers of America,* he listed the locations of twenty-two other similar maps.

When only one copy of an old map suddenly appears without precedent, its authenticity is immediately questioned. However, when several old maps like this exist, it reinforces that this style is not a recent invention suddenly thrown onto the market. The question then shifts to, "What does this map signify?"

Some contend that *Tian Xia (Ch'onhado)* maps support the theory that the Chinese reached the Americas by sea long before Columbus. Philippe Buache, a French geographer, started a heated debate in Europe in 1753 when he published a paper in Paris claiming (based on a Chinese text) that Chinese people had established in AD 458 a colony on the coast of California in a region called Fu Sang that Buache placed at about 55° north latitude.[12]

Buache had been discussing research of M. de Guignes, who then finally published in 1761 "Investigation of the Navigations of the Chinese to the Coast of America and Some Tribes Situated at the Eastern Extremity of Asia."[13] Perhaps de Guignes, remembering how Galileo had been persecuted in the previous century for his new ideas, was slow in coming forth with this unconventional information.

Arguments on this issue continued to arise then subside over the next several decades. Then, in 1843, the Chevalier de Paravey (a French nobleman) wrote an article titled "America under the Name of the Country of Fu-sang" in which he described Chinese world maps made prior to Matteo Ricci's that he had first seen in Oxford in 1830. He stated that these showed Fu Sang, which he contended was America, to the east of China.

> All the maps, rough and purposely altered as to the size of foreign countries, that we have been able to find in the books or collections relating to China, and anterior in date to the exact maps of the Celestial Empire, which were finally made by the aid of the corrections of the missionaries [Ricci] at Pekin [sic], show in fact to the east and northeast of China, beyond Japan, marked under one of its names, Ji pen ("Origin of the Sun"), a confused mass of countries, delineated as small islands, undoubtedly because they were reached by sea; and among these countries, of which the size is purposely reduced, is marked the celebrated country of Fu-sang, a country of which many fables have been related in China, but which, in the account translated by M. de Guignes, is presented in a light so entirely natural that it can not be considered otherwise than as one of the countries of America, even if it is not, as we think possible, intended for the entire Continent of America.[14]

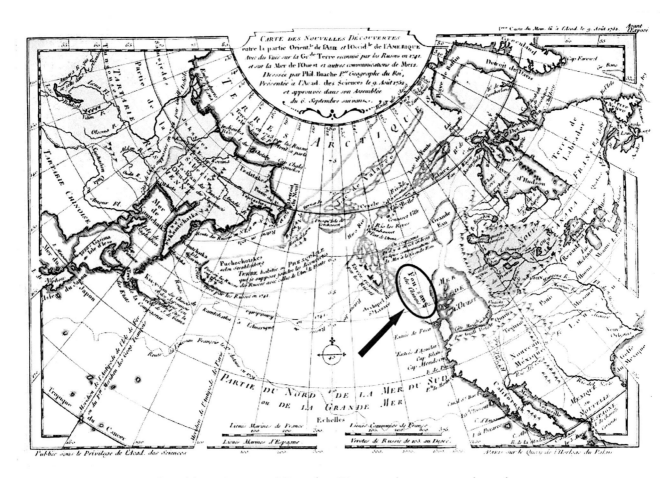

Buach's 1753 map - Note that 'Fou-sang' is annotated on the
American West Coast (arrow and circle by author).

M. de Paravey indicated that those Chinese pre-Ricci maps showed—in addition to America—Europe and all of Asia outside China. It appears from this article that they contained much of the same information as on the *Tian Xia* maps. If de Paravey were indeed referring to *Tian Xia* maps, what he designated as the "confused mass of countries delineated as small islands" were not islands at all, but were legends pertaining to the continents.

From these accounts above we know that since at least 1753, *before* the official founding of the United States of America in 1776, scholars have been arguing that there is evidence that the Chinese reached the Americas at pre-Columbian dates. In that debate, maps were considered.

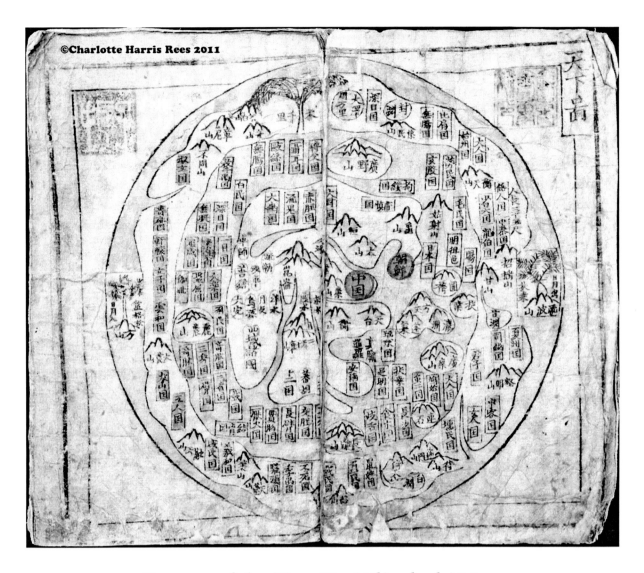

Features of the *Tian Xia (Ch'onhado)* Maps

The central land mass represents Asia, Africa, and Europe.

No expert disagrees that China, Korea, and Japan are shown in the center of the *Tian Xia* maps. On the first *Tian Xia* map my father saw, *Harris World Map 5*, the bottom red circle is China, the red circle above it Korea. With Asia in perspective, move west on the map. At the far left (west) bottom side of the center landmass, one sees Africa hanging down.

H. B. Hulbert, author of the acclaimed 1905 *The History of Korea,* mistook Africa calling it India.[15] However, when one compares Africa on the *Tian Xia* map to that continent on the 1402 *Kangnido* map (which shows both the eastern and western sides of Africa and Europe), one can see clearly that it is Africa. Above Africa is the Mediterranean Ocean (with no outlet to the Atlantic). Above that is Europe.

The outer land ring is the Americas cut in two.

With Asia, Europe, and Africa in perspective, one can see that the landmasses on the outer ring are the two coasts of the Americas divided roughly in half. The West Coast of America is on the far right side of the map, the East Coast to the left.

Several have asked, "How can theAmericas be depicted as a ring?" Easily—when one looks at a globe while focusing on the Pacific Ocean off the West Coast of the Americas. One will see that North and South America, with Antarctica, indeed form almost a half circle. It is a matter of perspective. Going due south from Chicago on longitudinal lines, one crosses Central America, but stays west of all of South America. South America arcs so far east that, even when going due south from Florida, one barely hits western South America.

For some it is more difficult to recognize the East Coast of the Americas on the *Tian Xia* configuration. Perhaps the early mapmakers conjectured that since the right side was portrayed as a half circle, then surely the left side of the map was similar.

Note this outline below of the current Chinese world map. All of North and South America are on the right side, but they circle around and almost join to Antarctica, which completes the arc.

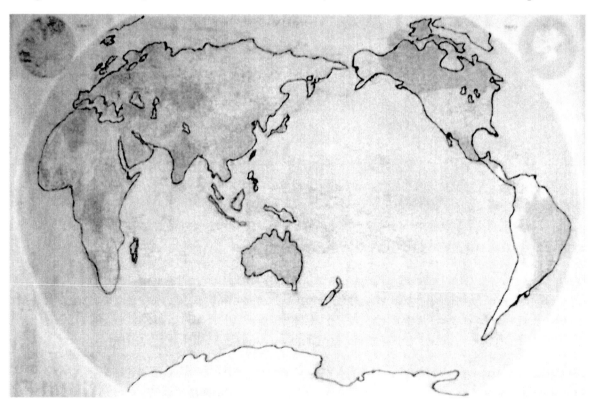

Outline of the current Chinese world map
with North and South America on the right side

After reading my father's original *The Asiatic Fathers of America,* David Deal drew the following illustration for me. I use it to explain how the outside land ring is actually the Americas cut in two.

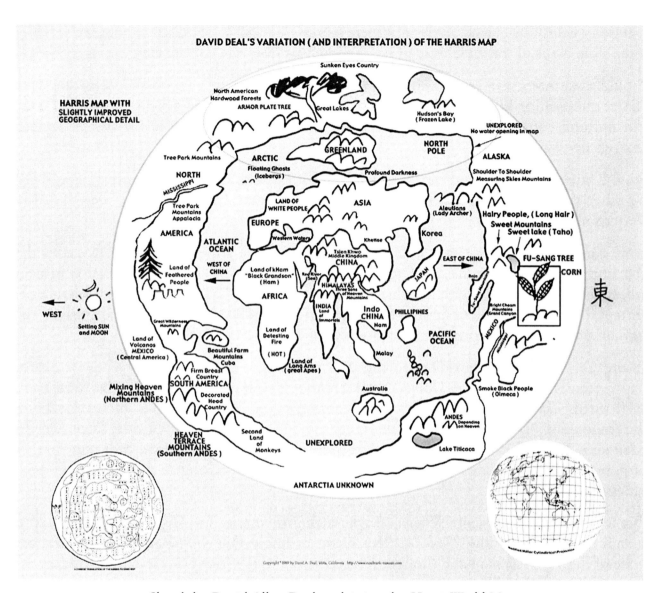

Sketch by David Allen Deal explaining the *Harris World Map*

The outer ring of land
represents the Americas divided.

In 1892, while *Ch'onhado* maps were still in use, Korean scholar Yi Ik Seup stated in *The Korean Repository* that both sides of the outer ring represented the Americas "divided so as to suit the flat surface."[16] Yi contended that the map had existed from "time immemorial."

After reading my manuscript of this book, Dr. Covey reinforced to me that if this were a court trial, Yi would be our primary witness concerning the meaning of the *Ch'onhado* maps. His testimony would be valued above all others because he was a reputable scholar, he was alive at the time maps of this style were in use, and he was from the culture that was using them.

Yi published more than one article in *The Korean Repository*. In a later issue, someone wrote a letter questioning his use of an English term in another unrelated article. However, I could find nothing contemporary to him disputing his contention that the *Ch'onhado* depicted America divided.

Unno Kazutaka of Japan and Bae Woo Sung of Korea, both of the 20th century, agreed that the outer ring represented the Americas, but thought that *Ch'onhado* maps were based on Western maps.[17]

Some Koreans today deny that *Ch'onhado* maps show the Americas at all. Oh stated that "the internal continent consists of real countries, but the internal sea, external continent, and external sea are filled with imaginary countries found in documents like Shanhaijing."[18] Perhaps it was just his lack of faith in the *Shan Hai Jing* and in the abilities of early sailors that prevented him from realizing that the "ring continent" was the Americas.

Kwang On Yoo of Chicago directed me to a photo of a derivation of a Japanese Sekisui map currently owned by the University of Southern Maine and thought to be from about 1850 titled, *Ten Thousand Country Map* **Mountain Sea Map** [emphasis mine] *Explained*. The "mountain" (shan) and "sea" (hai) are the same characters as those in the *Shan Hai Jing (Mountain Seas Classic)*. A statement on the legend on this Sekisui map indicates that the purpose of this document was to make it easy for children looking at this and the globe to understand the world.[19]

This is a startling statement. What else would the *Mountain Sea Map* that they wanted to explain be—except for the *Tian Xia*. This seems to imply that the Japanese of that era were aware of the *Tian Xia* map and thought it important enough to explain to schoolchildren as a real world map—just like the Sekisui map, which clearly shows the Americas.

The outer "ocean" indicates where earth and sky meet.

People have asked, "What does the outer circle of 'water' on this map represent?" Yi Ik Seup stated in 1892 that the flat earth on these maps was "hooked into eternity in some way by the corners."[20]

If on a picture of a *Tian Xia* map one cuts off the round outer blue region, the external land mass remaining (the ring continent) actually forms more of a square than a circle. Early Chinese believed that the earth was square and the sky round. "The gaitian (covered heaven) theory posited the earth as square-shaped bowl, turned upside down and covered by a hemispherical dome. The heavens were said to be 'round, like an umbrella,' while the earth was described as 'square, like a chessboard.'"[21]

I believe that the outer ring of blue on the *Tian Xia* was not meant to be another ocean but rather the horizon—where the square earth met the round sky.[22] Oh stated that "the drawing of heaven and earth in the outer ring of the circle appears to be an attempt to express yin and yang, or the balance of heaven and earth."[23]

Though Ledyard did not note the possibility of the outer ring being the sky, he mentioned that none of these old maps (except for the one at the British Library) shows islands in that outer ring. He stated that the three trees depicted on them sometimes extend into that outer ring, but seem to sprout from the adjacent land.[24] We all know that trees do sprout from land and reach into the sky. After all, *tian*, which means heaven or sky, is part of the title of the *Tian Xia* map.

Most of the "islands" in the inner ocean are legends, not islands.

Some people become confused because they see what they believe to be many "islands" in the inner ocean of this world map. My father pointed out that these are not islands at all but are legends referring to the mainland.

Ledyard referred to them as "cartouches." Most are basically the same size and shape—depending on which map one views. There are also a few landmasses of different shapes in that ocean. Some believe that the boomerang shaped object in the middle of the Pacific depicts Australia.

That the width of the ocean is not to scale suggests an early date for the origin of this map.

Strange location names do not preclude these from being real countries.

Perhaps part of the quandary regarding the *Tian Xia* maps comes from the fact that many of the countries shown have strange names. Nakamura demonstrated that 110 out of 145 place names on the map are from the Chinese geography the *Shan Hai Jing*.[25] Therefore, some who view the *Shan Hai Jing* as fantasy or who perceive the names as too fabulous, think that these countries on the map cannot be real.

Most of the place names on this map
are from the Chinese *Shan Hai Jing.*

Whatever strange name a country was given by a non-resident does not deny the fact that the land was there. Years ago when my mother and I were on a tour, our guide was harsh, so behind her back we called her "dragon lady." That was never her real name and, of course, she was not a dragon. Our referring to her by that fantastic name did not preclude her from being a real person.

古天下圖
Ancient World Map
何盛頓藏
Dr. Hendon Harris Collection

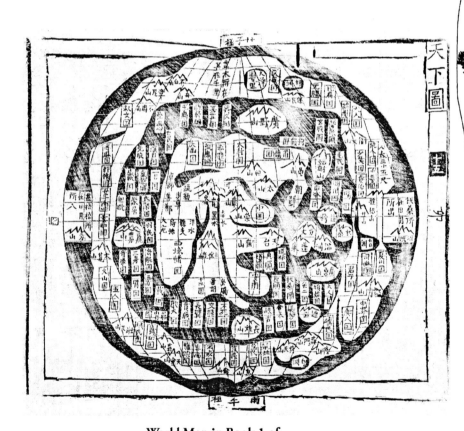

World Map in Book 1 of
Dr. Hendon Harris Map Collection

English Translation
of Harris Map

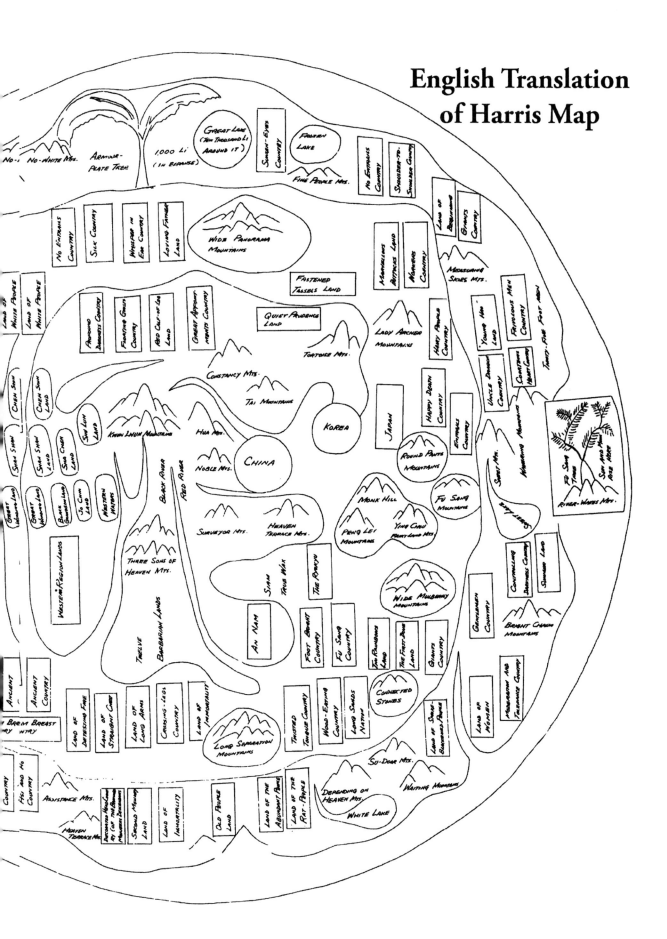

No one debates that the countries in the middle of this style map—China, Japan, Korea, etc.—are real countries. However, *The History of Cartography* and several other sources, while calling this a "world map," claim that it is part real and part imaginary. They say that other than China and a few surrounding countries, the rest are imaginary—but are they?

Since all other maps in the *Harris Map Collection* are confirmed as genuine and serious, why would the *Tian Xia* map be otherwise? Some of the *Harris Map Books* were surely at one time owned by government officials because they contain state secrets of that day. What purpose would be served by including imaginary maps in such books? That would be like including *Cat in the Hat* in the *Congressional Record*!

The unusual location names (toponyms) on this map are discussed in more detail in *The Asiatic Fathers of America* and *Secret Maps of the Ancient World*. On the east side of the map is Fu Sang in approximately the vicinity of California. Hui Shun had reported to the Chinese court that Fu Sang was situated 20,000 li or more to the East of China. He also reported the Land of Women in that vicinity. Early Spanish explorers also reported a Land of Women in the area of California.[26]

In *The Asiatic Fathers of America* Harris discussed many of the strange names on this map. Below are some of his comments about toponyms on the right side of the map:

- **Fu Sang** – Three times we see the land on the extreme right (East) of the map designated Fu Sang. Fu Sang Mountains, Fu Sang Forest, and Fu Sang Continent appear indicated. We can have no doubt we are dealing with West Coast America.

- **Land of Beginning** is Alaska. Since Fu Sang is the center, the eastern side of the map is plainly the beginning of the Fu Sang area.

- **Hairy People Land** is near Land of Beginning – these [hairy people] are probably Eskimos.

- **Equal to Heaven Mountain** (Measuring Skies Mountain) is probably Mt. McKinley – the highest peak in North America.

- **Chasm of the Bright Mountains** is at the spot where the Grand Canyon of the Colorado is found. Several hundred miles east of modern Los Angeles are the Low Bright Mountains. The only place in the world where there are famous mountains that are very bright and yet beneath the earth's surface are the Low Bright Mountains. Their presence on the map is immediate confirmation of the 4200 year old stories about Fu Sang in the Chinese *Book of Mountains and the Seas* – the *Shan Hai Jing*. Every person who has visited the place where the mountains are hidden in the bowels of the earth will recognize this place as the Grand Canyon. Here is the river that went to form the beautiful gulf told about so long ago by the Chinese.

- **Gentlemen Country** – We find this land in the area between modern Los Angeles and San Francisco. [He wrote that ke qi means "polite" in Mandarin. Therefore, he believed that these polite gentlemen became the Cochise – which is pronounced almost the same as ke qi.]

- **Decorated Head Country** is found in the Yucatan. The French copy of this map even shows Yucatan on the Pacific with the Decorated people there. The long [elongated] and decorated heads are exactly what were found among the leadership class in Maya land.

- **The Land of Hsi and Ho** – the [abode] of the astronomers from China is in Central America. It fits perfectly with the traditions and history of that land. [Pyramids positioned to indicate solstices].

Harris wrote concerning the **Land of Women** on his map:

> The Land of the Women was right next to the Southern Hopi tribe at the side of the gulf of Baja, on the Eastern shore. This is the country for which Hui Shun was ridiculed in the days of Emperor Liang Wu Ti in 502 A.D. When he told the court reporters that there was a land of women in Fu Sang. . . . the Land of Women gives us a physical point of reference from which we can find our way north, south, east and west. It is the Rosetta Stone of the Hui Shun account and unlocks all the geographical doors. In this area were found slant eyed figurines with an East Indian turban-type hairdress. . . . Alfred E. Johnson mentions the many temporary midden [refuse heap] sites along the coast of the gulf of Baja, and the preponderance of female figurines found there.[27]

The three trees give direction and also indicate the sequoia.

Three trees shown on many of these maps are most likely there to give orientation. On the right side of the map is "Fu Sang Tree," then "Sun and moon rise here." Written on the left side of the map is "Pan Ke Pine" and "Sun and moon set here." The tree at the top of the map is marked "Armor plate tree." See my article titled "Ancient Chinese wrote about America's Big Trees" in the addendum of this book.

McCune thought that these trees might be Buddhist symbols. He stated that they are not on the later *Ch'onhado* of the 19th century when Buddhism was out of favor in Korea.[28]

Five of the *Harris World Maps* display the three trees. This may help date these five as older.

I was told by a professor with a PhD in Environmental Studies that the Fu Sang tree depicted on *Harris Map 5* has the configuration of the needles of the gigantic sequoia trees found in California. Hulbert stated in a review of the *Ch'onhado* that, according to the legend of Fu Sang, "In that country grew enormous trees, 400 feet in height. Some people think this refers to America; and it certainly matches the facts very well."[29]

If Chinese reached America early, surely they would have encountered the large trees on the West Coast. Vining wrote that in the third century BC, Tong Fan Tso, an author in China, discussed the enormous trees in Fu Sang. Tso's dimensions for Fu Sang almost match the exact width and height of North America. Furthermore, he contended that another big blue ocean lay to the east of Fu Sang.

The Fu Sang Tree on the right side of the map is a Sequoia.

Tso was clearly impressed with the trees in Fu Sang but his descriptions of them were surely hyperbole. He contended that the trees grew to several times ten thousand cubits, and that it took two thousand people to reach their arms around one of them.

Hulbert also indicated that the mapmakers wrote "Fu Sang" three times on the right side of the *Ch'onhado*. Therefore, he thought they were unsure of the exact location of Fu Sang.[30] Oh brings out that Mt. Yupa is included in the map legend by the Fu Sang tree, but that in its actual location on that atlas, Mt. Yupa has no sacred tree and is a long distance away from that legend.[31]

My father believed that Fu Sang was mentioned three times because it was a large area.[32] He also pointed out that Tso indicated that Fu Sang was 10,000 (Chinese) li (about 3,300 miles) upon each of its sides and had enormous trees.[33] Perhaps inclusion of Mt. Yupa on the legend reinforces that Fu Sang was expansive, much as inclusion of the sequoia frond locates it in North America.

Longitude and latitude lines are on some editions of these maps.

Some writers contend that some of the *Ch'onhado* have "false graticule"—incorrectly placed latitude and longitude lines. Perhaps it is considered false because the maps are not to scale.

That these lines were added to some of the *Ch'onhado* maps is understandable but does not necessarily make them more recent. However, since this style of map is not to scale, those lines would have little meaning other than to suggest that the map was based on a real world, not an imaginary one. McCune stated that "the supposed geodetic grid [longitude and latitude] gave an aura of authenticity to a world map with many fictitious names."[34]

McCune believed that mapmakers started making maps with grids in the 19th century. He based his argument for that date on the fact that Verbiest's world map was produced in a Korean wood block edition in 1860.[35]

Ferdinand Verbiest, a Belgian Jesuit missionary, had produced his map in China around 1674. Modern world maps showing longitude and latitude circulated in Korea starting with Ricci in the early 17th century. Therefore, Koreans were well aware of maps with coordinates before

1860. However, McCune was correct in that these lines were late additions to the *Ch'onhado* style maps.

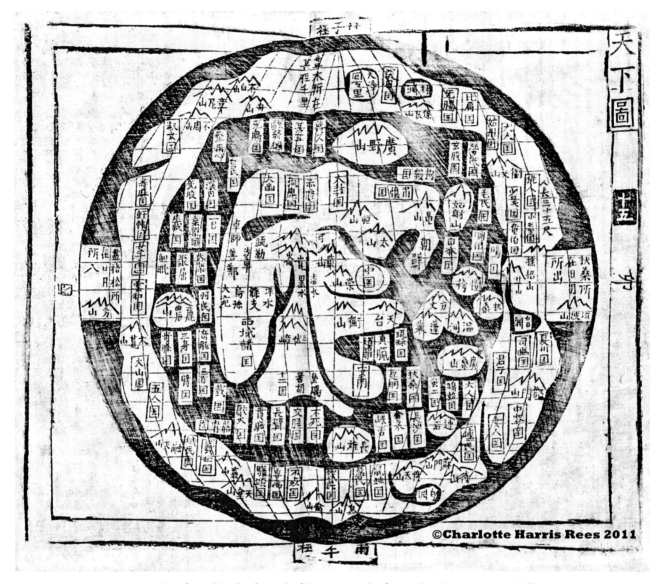

An example of a *Ch'onhado* with false graticule from the *Harris Map Collection*

The Religious and Philosophical Influence on These Maps

Though these *Ch'onhado* maps circulated widely in Korea from the 17th century right up to the end of the 19th, it is a wonder that they were used there at all. They appear to be based on Taoist beliefs that were much less influential in Korea than in China.[36] McCune wrote: "The outermost border is often a representation of the Yang-Yin symbols so prevalent in the Far East."[37]

McCune then mentioned possible Buddhist influence from a prior era. Buddhism reached China approximately 2,000 years ago, and Buddhists did use those symbols. Asians, including Buddhists, frequently commingled religions. However, the concept of yin and yang originated with Taoist beliefs that some date back to the Yellow Emperor, who even pre-dated Yu the

Great (2000 BC). Therefore, some of what McCune interpreted as Buddhist may actually have been Taoist.

The yin yang symbol has long been used both
by Asians and some Native Americans.

Bagrow wrote that "Taoism held that China occupied only 1/81 of the earth's surface and was surrounded by an ocean, beyond which were other countries, separated by concentric rings of ocean."[38]

McCune cited Nakamura's 1966 article in French. McCune stated that in that translation of Nakamura's previous article, he showed a photo of a *Ch'onhado* that he had seen in Korea in the Museum of the Government General of Chosen (No. 9734). Nakamura contended that it was "very similar to a Chinese map from *T'u-shu-pien*, a Chinese encyclopedia compiled by Chinese scholar Chang Huang . . . in the period 1562-1577 and was derived from a Buddhist map of earlier date."[39] Chang annotated that he had copied his map from a Buddhist map.

Korean Buddhist monk-scholars made pilgrimages to China during the Koryo Dynasty (918-1392). "In the epitaph of a Korean scholar who died in 1154 it is noted that he made and presented to the Koryo court a copy of a well-known Buddhist map, the *Map of the Five Indies*, based in part on the travels of a Chinese Buddhist monk."[40] However, none of the maps of the Koryo period still exist.

Others deny that these maps are Buddhist because they do not include any Buddhist place names. Oh stated:

> It is impossible that a map representing the Buddhist worldview would circulate among Confucian scholars in a society dominated by Neo-Confucianism[41] [as Korea of that era was] . . . . the Shanhaijing was . . . treated as a heretical book by

Confucians who stressed practicality and realism. . . . Shanhaijing was regarded as a strange book even by Chinese Confucian scholars.[42]

We suspect that the maps were from an earlier era, and perhaps simply passed through Buddhist hands. The concepts on this map had to have come from a pre-Confucian era.

Perhaps their popularity at late dates in Korea was fanned by the isolationism of that era. Koreans knew there were other countries, but perhaps felt more comfortable with old maps that depicted foreigners as strange and far away.

Tian Xia (Ch'onhado) Maps May Indicate Sea Travel

These round maps are real. The sides of the ring continent are the Americas. However, I believe that they portray more. During one of my PowerPoint speeches I looked up at the large image on the screen and stopped in my tracks. I was discussing the ocean currents of the world while looking at an image furnished by the US National Oceanic and Atmospheric Administration (NOAA).[72] Suddenly I realized that their drawing is very similar to the configuration of the *Harris World Map*.

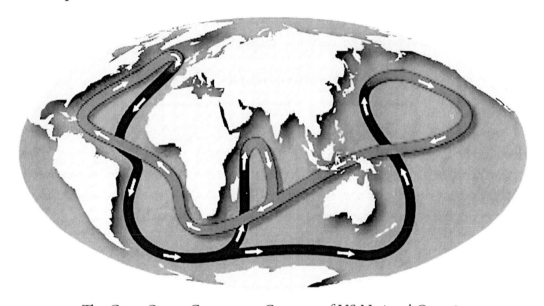

The Great Ocean Conveyor—Courtesy of US National Oceanic
and Atmospheric Administration

Though this National Oceanic and Atmospheric Administration map is centered on India, it shows North America divided—simply because that is the best way to demonstrate the interconnecting global ocean currents. However, were the center of this NOAA map moved east to China, it would still indicate the currents while showing part of South America and more of North America on the right side of the map—as the *Tian Xia* map does. Therefore, I believe that the *Tian Xia*, like the NOAA map, was made this way to indicate travel via ocean currents.

Does the *Tian Xia* Map Have Current Implications Concerning Global Warming?

Philip Mulholland, a professional geoscientist with an international company, wrote:

> The latest news giving details of the Harris Map collection is truly astonishing. The maps collected by Dr. Harris and identified by him as a representation of the legendary Fu Sang, now known as America, are very significant. These maps vastly extend the time frame of Chinese knowledge of the world and place the explorations of Zheng He in an historic and cultural context of continuous and refined geographical knowledge.

> This new early map, as explained by David Deal, shows that although both the Pacific west coast and the Atlantic east coast of America were known and placed in their correct positions with respect to China, the Southern Ocean connection between the Pacific and Atlantic Oceans (the Drake Passage) was not known and that southern hemisphere circumnavigation had not yet been achieved. . . .

The *Tian Xia* map shows an ice-free sea passage across the Arctic Ocean.

> What is, however, of equal or indeed greater significance is the knowledge of the Arctic Ocean and certainly of its navigation from Europe to China as the most feasible route home from eastern North America. The implications of open ice-free sea passage across the Arctic Ocean 4,000 years ago suggest that the current polar sea ice variations are not historically unusual.

Did the Aztecs of North America Have Knowledge of a Map Like This?

The Aztec people had many characteristics similar to the Chinese. Their concept of the world was that it was a round flat disc surrounded by water. Could they have seen a map like the *Tian Xia* before and not understood its meaning?

Chapter 5

The *Tian Xia* (*Ch'onhado*)
"Everything Under Heaven" World Map
Country of Origin and Date

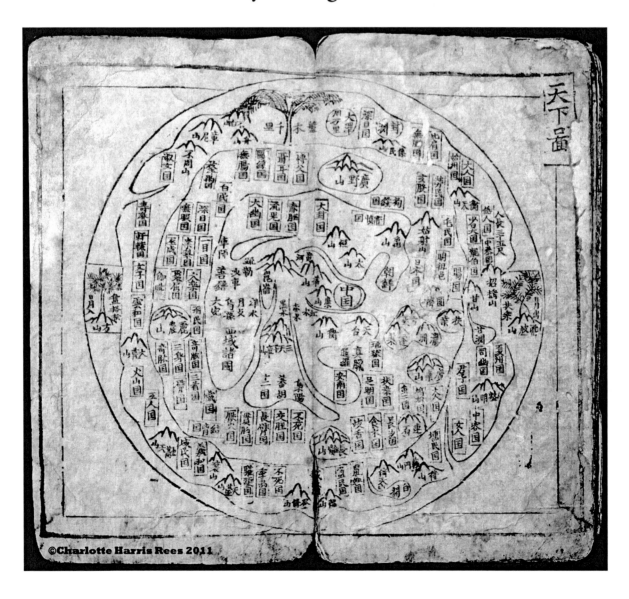

Where Did *Tian Xia* Maps Originate?

Argument for Western origin

Some believe that those who created the *Ch'onhado* maps were influenced by single-circle Western maps, including Ricci's. Those who believe this accept the outer continent as North and South America.[43]

Arguments for Korean Origin

Korean map expert, Lee Chan, while arguing for a Korean origin of the map, stated that "the map is a traditionally sinocentric world map with no substantial influence of Ricci's map in its content or in the shapes of the land."[44]

Though he listed the Chinese documents from which this map was believed to have descended, McCune thought that the *Ch'onhado* itself was Korean.[45]

Oh, unaware of similar maps made outside Korea, claimed that this style map was "produced solely in Korea."[46] He found it "unreasonable to seek the origin of circular world maps in Western circular world maps"[47] since the Western maps have no external continent and do not have corresponding place names.

Richard J. Smith contended that the 1402 Korean map, the *Kangnido*, inspired the *Ch'onhado*.[48]

Yi Ik Seup believed the *Ch'onhado* was of Korean origin. Though Yi was the primary witness to the meaning of the map, what he knew concerning the origin of the map was only hearsay because he, like the rest of us, was not present at the time it was first drawn. In this instance, the least biased witnesses may be those who have no nationalistic or ulterior interests invested in where it originated.

Indications of Chinese Origin

Nakamura of Japan, while acknowledging that most of the *Tian Xia* maps that he had seen were Korean, wrote of one published in Japan and seemed certain that all the maps had descended from the Chinese.[49]

Needham shows a *Tian Xia* map and mentions examples shown in ancient Chinese texts. Needham stated, "There can be no reason for doubting that the Koreans received this tradition from China, though it seems never to have been so popular there [in China]."[50]

Although he espoused Korean origin himself, Oh noted that "Ogawa Takuji [Japanese] . . . assumed them to be *Shanhaijing [Shan Hai Jing]* maps."[51] (Of course, the *Shan Hai Jing* is Chinese.)

Oh noted that the *Shan Hai Jing* presents the world in three parts—the inner continent, the seas, and the outer continent: "The image of the world as a series of concentric circles . . . is found in such ancient documents as *Shanhaijing* . . . . This series of concentric circles is based on ancient Chinese understanding of geography, and thus closely linked to Sinocentrism."[52]

The *Shan Hai Jing* gives directions for where the countries should be, and the countries are in those locations. Oh noted that "there is a strong possibility that the concentric circle format of circular world maps originated from documents like *Shanhaijing* rather than from other maps that existed earlier."[53] However, Oh stated: "It could not have been created without reference to other maps."[54]

In *Chinese Maps: Images of 'All Under Heaven,'* Richard J. Smith displays one map of this round style that he says is Chinese.[55]

Ledyard contends that at one time the word ch'onhado was used to designate maps of China.[56] Ledyard wrote: "during the Ming (1368-1644) particularly, Koreans commonly referred to maps of China as ch'onhado or some close variation."[57]

Did maps of the same name signify something different only a few years earlier? Would not use of this same title for maps of China suggest Chinese origin of the *Ch'onhado* world map? Could the title designate both "maps of China" and "maps belonging to China"?

My friends Randy and Sandy Beaty lived in China for several years. On one of his trips back to China, Randy took a copy of *Secret Maps of the Ancient World* and loaned it to his friend James Zhang who grew up near Xi'an. After reading the book, James told Randy that prior to the Cultural Revolution, many families in China had similar map books that had been handed down for generations. He believed, however, that most were destroyed during the Cultural Revolution.

When is the Origin Date of *Tian Xia* Maps?

Traditionally *Tian Xia* maps are undated and unsigned. As in the case of most ancient documents, the original *Tian Xia* map, so far as we know, is no longer in existence.

Yi Ik Seup contended that this style was from "time immemorial." Bagrow stated: "The world-map is a relic of very early times."[58]

In *The History of Cartography,* Ledyard states regarding the *Tian Xia (Ch'onhado),* that the map made a "silent and utterly unnoted debut at a date we cannot pin even to the century,[59] [and that]. . . . this distinctive world map did not spring up out of whole cloth in the sixteenth century. It had much earlier sources and these are best approached through a study of the place names." Ledyard then points out that 72 percent of the location names on this style map are derived from the Chinese *Shan Hai Jing.*[60]

While some debate the date of origin of the *Shan Hai Jing,* it is repeatedly attributed to Yu of the first Chinese dynasty (about 2000 BC) and was quoted throughout Chinese history.

Ledyard stated that Hao Yixing (China, 1747-1825) and others believed that maps originally accompanied the *Shan Hai Jing*[61]—but those maps are long gone. If *Tian Xia* maps descended from them, it would put the origin date at about 2000 BC.

My father believed that his and other similar maps descended from those extremely early *Shan Hai Jing* maps[62]—and thus were copies of many generations of copies. Because of various occasions of political turmoil and/or times when China shut itself off from the rest of the world and forbade sea travel (as in the early 15th century), Father reasoned that the maps had not survived in China, but had lived on in neighboring Korea.

However, Oh argued that no maps of this style are known to be older than the 17th century. He wrote: "Based on analysis of existing copies of circular world maps, the prevailing view is that they were made in the seventeenth century or thereafter. No circular world atlases or folders believed to have been made earlier have been uncovered."[63] His article admitted that if any maps had been produced earlier they could have been lost. He stated that maps of this style continued to be produced until the late 19th century.

Lee Chan in *Old Maps of Korea* published by the Korea Library Science Research Institute, stated that in the early Yi (Choson) Dynasty (1392-1910), this map and the *Kangnido*, produced in 1402, were both in use. Lee contended:

> Two different types of world maps can be found in the early period of the Yi Dynasty. One is a world map based on scientific geographical knowledge of that time, and the other is an abstract one manifesting the imaginative worldview of that time. The former is *Honil-gangni-yokdae-kukdo-chi* [*Kangnido*] and the latter is the round world map *Ch'onhado* (World Map: Map of all under heaven).[64]

(The 17th century date that Oh proposes above is a long time after the early Yi claimed by Lee.)

Kim Yangson (a prominent Korean archaeologist and historian who died in 1971), citing similar map titles mentioned in Korean texts, believed that this style was being used in the 14th and 15th centuries.

McCune believed that based on all the maps in the *Ch'onhado* atlases that they started being used in Korea about two decades before AD 1500.

Nakamura of Japan argued that this style map had Chinese beginnings earlier than the Tang Dynasty (AD 618).[65]

The oldest example of a *Tian Xia* map is in a Chinese book.

Needham, in *Science and Civilisation in China,* cites Chinese works of 1562 and 1607 that show this style map.[66] If Oh, referenced above, is correct in stating that no Korean maps of this style older than the 17th century still exist, then the Chinese map mentioned by Needham in the 1562 *Thu Shu Pien (On Maps and Books)* by Chang Huang predates all similar Korean examples of this map.

Furthermore, Needham traces a clear verbal description of a *Tian Xia* map to a Chinese author of the Chin Dynasty (AD 266-316) who mentioned an incident involving this style map in the first year of the Shang Dynasty (1766 BC) when the emperor wanted to see it.[67] (The map discussed in that text had several similar details, including "concentric zones" and the "Fu-Sang tree.")

Ledyard quoted Zou Yan, a third century BC Chinese philosopher who wrote: "'As for the sea around China in the four directions, I call it 'the tiny sea' [bihai]. Beyond that sea there is a great continent that rings it, and beyond the great continent there is a vast ocean sea circling around. It is only there [that one comes to] the edge of the earth.'"[68] This certainly appears to be a description of this style map.

Recent texts mention the *Tian Xia* map. In *Mapping the World,* published in 2006, Michael Swift calls it a "Chinese World Map of 1500."[69]

In the 2007 *Cartographia: Mapping Civilizations,* co-authors Vincent Virga and the Library of Congress conveniently placed the date at 1592. That book states:

> Then Japan in quest of empire attacked in 1592. During this period of great turmoil the *Ch'onhado* appeared. Mysterious in its origins and tenacious in its grip on the Korean collective imagination, it is a relic bearing a very early Chinese mental organization of the world . . . . It is believed to have 'evolved' from the *Kangnido*, though the integrated known world has been 'exploded,' like a myth, and China returned to center stage as the Middle Kingdom.[70]

It is incredible what Virga as well as the Geography and Maps Division of the Library of Congress implied by that statement. While his country was being attacked by Japan, the Korean mapmaker did not run for cover, but apparently had a vision. He sat down and drew a relatively accurate map that put China, not Korea, at center stage. He drew lands that were there, even though he had never been to them nor had been allowed to visit. He drew them according to how ancient Chinese had viewed the world, which was contrary to contemporary Korean thought. He meticulously listed the countries where the *Shan Hai Jing* said they would be.

Of course, the staff of the Library of Congress has access to all the sources that I quote. Previously they told me that the *History of Cartography* was the "Bible" regarding maps. That text could not even name the century the *Ch'onhado* had originated. However, suddenly Virga and the Library staff knew more than their "Bible."

In *Cartographia: Mapping Civilizations,* the authors state that, "near the eastern tree is the land of 'Pusang,' [Fu Sang] which may be America."[71] Was the reason that Virga and the Library of Congress chose 1592 because they feared that this was a real world map that showed America? Placing the date earlier than Columbus could have political repercussions. This date (1592) conveniently put the origin of the *Ch'onhado* exactly 100 years after Columbus' arrival to the Americas.

In 2008, Dr. Hwa-Wei Lee, the retired Chief of the Asian Division of the Library of Congress and Dean Emeritus of Ohio University Libraries, gave strong endorsement for my publication of *Secret Maps of the Ancient World*. Dr. Lee, a distinguished librarian and scholar, echoed my findings that there is much evidence that Chinese had travelled by sea and by land to the Americas long before Columbus. He strongly encouraged the publication of my research and findings so as to generate more scholarly studies by using a variety of approaches and an abundance of resources.

If Koreans made the *Ch'onhado* from maps acquired from the Chinese, those Chinese surveys had to have been made prior to 1433 when China shut down to the outside world. After that date, sea travel was banned. Therefore, if Chinese made the maps before 1433, then they arrived in the Americas before Columbus.

Furthermore, the accurate details of the West Coast of the Americas that appeared on later European maps and in Ricci's map before European exploration of those locations all had to have come from Chinese surveys made well before 1433. However, as I explain in detail in *Secret Maps of the Ancient World*, there is much evidence that those Chinese surveys and maps came much earlier than that.

Conclusions

There has been and continues to be much debate about the *Tian Xia (Ch'onhado)* style of map. Recently more people recognize this as a real world map and acknowledge that it indicates the Americas. At the same time, many of those same scholars have now shifted to later dates of the map's origin. When it was part imaginary, it was easier to accept the earlier dates. Seemingly, they just cannot allow that perhaps Chinese people or anyone from Asia reached the Americas by sea before Columbus.

I believe that those proposing the origin date of the *Ch'onhado* as 17th century are ignoring history. In Korea this was a period of isolationism—of purposely embracing the old and rejecting the new. At that time, Koreans used the map because it was old. By then, private citizens were allowed to own maps—a luxury previously out of the question.

Why is it so difficult for some to admit the obvious—that *all* parts of this map were real and descended from a map that at some time the Koreans acquired from the Chinese? Chinese, Korean, and some Japanese traits are found among Native American tribes. Perhaps Koreans and Japanese accompanied the Chinese on some of the ancient voyages. The map probably did not survive in China because of the ban placed on sea travel in 1433 after Zheng He's final voyage, but did in Korea because they embraced the old.

To me this is a real life *DaVinci Code* type situation—with the truth hidden in plain sight.

Carrying this thought forward, I pondered that if ancient Chinese had really traveled the world, they would have used the ocean currents they wrote about. Were maps of this style actually drawn this way because they were originally primitive sailing charts?

Owl shaped antique Chinese clay tripod pitcher from the collection of
Hendon Mason Harris Jr., - courtesy of Aurora Dawn Harris.

Chapter 6

Other Maps that Relate to the
Tian Xia (Ch'onhado) Atlases

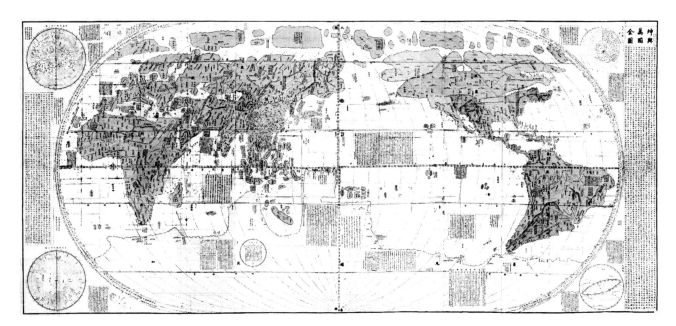

The 1602 *Map of the Ten Thousand Countries of the Earth*

The 1602 *Map of Ten Thousand Countries of the Earth*

The 1602 map, the third of Ricci's Chinese world maps, is the most well known. Its inauguration created controversy in China because that country is not positioned at the exact center of this map. Therefore, some Chinese felt slighted, thinking that they had been displaced from the center of the world.[1]

While only indirectly related to the *Tian Xia* map, the 1602 map has recently garnered much media attention. An excellent photo of this map suitable for zoom in and study can be viewed online.[2] Lee Chan states that a copy of Matteo Ricci's 1602 map had reached Korea in 1603.[3]

This map was put together from both Chinese and Western sources.[4] Some claim that it is based on a projection of the world developed by Ortelius.[5] It is an understatement to say that Ricci's map looks very different from Ortelius's map.

When we recall the copy of the *Tian Xia* map in the 1562 Chinese book, which we discussed it Chapter 4, we realize that there is solid proof that the *Tian Xia* map preceded the 1602 map. Thus it is likely that the *Tian Xia* along with Ortelius were used in tandem as models from which the 1602 map emerged. Further support for *Tian Xia* as a model is that some of the *Shan Hai Jing* countries, including the Land of Women, appear on the 1602 map.[6]

In early 2010, the Library of Congress touted Ricci's 1602 map as "the first map in Chinese to show the Americas."[7] At the end of this book see my rebuttal to that pronouncement, which I sent as an e-mail titled, "Is the Library of Congress Hiding Information?"

Based on a significant amount of evidence that I had previously shared with the Geography and Maps division of the Library of Congress, I contended that the *Tian Xia* map shows the Americas, is also in Chinese, and was earlier than Ricci's map. Furthermore, I stated that the Library seemed to be blocking promotion of evidence they possess that shows Chinese preceded Columbus to the Americas. I received supportive comments back from people on every continent but Antarctica.

The University of Minnesota has an original of Ricci's 1602 map, owned by the James Ford Bell Trust. It was printed from wooden blocks on six paper scrolls—each measuring 1820 x 3650 mm (approximately 2 feet by 5.75 feet). Informally known as the 1602 Matteo Ricci map, the official title is *Kunyu wanguo quantu (Map of the Ten Thousand Countries of the Earth)*. Because it was so rare, it was also known as "The Impossible Black Tulip."

The University of Minnesota wrote:

> Li Zhizao . . . was the Chinese cartographer who engraved the map. It was printed by Zhang Wentao of Hangzhou, probably an official printer of the Ming court.
>
> A Jesuit priest, Matteo Ricci arrived in China in 1583 and, with fellow Jesuit Michele Ruggieri, established the first Christian mission. . . . His world map is a true collaboration between the European scholars of the Jesuit mission and the Chinese scholars of the imperial court. Vivid descriptions of the continents, praise of the Chinese emperor, lunar charts, and scientific tables documenting the movement of the planets adorn the map, a unique representation of East-West relations in the early 17th century.[8]

Though Ricci has long received sole credit for introducing the Chinese people to the world via this map, it is good to see that the University of Minnesota also recognizes the Chinese contribution to this document. Others and I have questioned how a European priest who had never been to North America could have in 1602 so accurately drawn parts of that continent that were not explored by Europeans until two centuries later.[9]

Dr. S. L. Lee of Ohio has researched this 1602 map extensively and contends that information written on it presents proof that the Chinese had visited and surveyed America and also circumnavigated the world well before Columbus.[10]

The 1602 map shows the Northwest and Northeast passages, Antarctica, and the Bering Strait hundreds of years before Europeans explored those locations.

Dr. Edward Lin of Florida communicated to me by e-mail regarding some interesting findings on this 1602 map. He stated:

> They named Canada, Chile, Cuba, and Jamaica phonetically in Chinese and substantially correct geographically. Ba ha ma (Bahamas) is clearly shown off the Florida peninsula. Deep in the upper tributaries of the Amazon River (which is not named as such on the map) is the designation "Amazon nation." To the north and west is a 3-letter word the first two of which sounded just like "Mayan" and the third word, "X," is a word I do not recognize and hints at an architectural structure. While it would be very tempting to think this relates in some way to a Mayan City or ruins, this location is quite far south from the Yucatan-Belize area where Mayan ruins are typically thought to be found.

Obviously there is still much study that needs to be done, but this opens several interesting questions. Unexplained ruins have been found in South America, such as those at Machu Picchu. In *Secret Maps of the Ancient World* I wrote that the *Tian Xia* maps show a second Land of Women in approximately the location of the Amazons and I discussed a 12th century Chinese text that seems to reference them. I also mentioned the possible Chinese derivation of the word "Amazon."

The 1602 Ricci map described horses and buffaloes on the US Great Plains over 200 years before Lewis and Clark explored there.

However, Dr. Lin's continued statement below about the 1602 Ricci map raised the most curiosity in me.

> Over the northwestern Great Plains it states: "In this area are numerous wild horses, and mountain buffaloes, which have a hump like that seen on the camel." Clearly they saw mustangs and herds of bison! Over the Alaska region, a notation is made that "The land here is so cold even the sea turns into ice. The people hunt giant fish because they cannot cultivate crops. The meat is consumed and the oil used for lamps." Apparently referring to whaling by Eskimos.

This map with these startling statements was produced in 1602. Jamestown, the first permanent English settlement in the new world, was not founded until 1607—five years after this map was made. Jamestown is in Virginia—on the East Coast. The famous explorers Lewis and

Clark made their trek from St. Louis, the middle of the continent, westward across the Great Plains, but not until 1804-1806. The Spanish and French were also exploring North America, but they did not get that far that early. So in 1602, how did Ricci, a Catholic Priest from Europe and living in China, know what was in North America in regions not yet explored by Westerners? Surely he was instructed by the Chinese.

Lam Yee Din, an independent researcher, points out that this 1602 map:

> does not use the European 90 degrees for latitude, but 91 degrees or more which represents Chinese 365.25 days per year divided by 4 . . . [the] Chinese characters for 90 degrees are not located on South Pole or North Pole [as we show them today] but are some distance [away] . . . . This further confirms that the map is based on Chinese latitude . . . therefore, it is believed that the map was copied directly from the source of a Chinese world map.

The 1402 *Kangnido*

On the Korean world map of 1402, the *Kangnido,* the size of Korea is greatly exaggerated, while Japan is shown in reduced scale and sideways.[11] In addition to Asia it shows both the eastern and western sides of Africa and Europe. However, it does not indicate the Americas.

According to Lee Chan, both the *Kangnido* and the *Ch'onhado* were in use in Korea during the early Joseon era. The fact that the primitive *Ch'onhado* shows the Americas and yet the more modern *Kangnido* does not, could suggest that in using the *Ch'onhado* the Koreans were using someone else's map which they did not fully comprehend.

Bae stated that Kwon Geun, a Korean official, wrote notes on the bottom of the original *Kangnido* that indicate that the Koreans got most of the information on that map from the Chinese. Therefore, we know for certain that at times Korea borrowed maps from China.

Bae contended: "According to Kwon's notes, Joseon obtained Li Zemin's world map *shengjiao guangbeitu* and Qingjun's *Hunyi jianglitu* [both Chinese], merged the two and added the maps of Joseon and Japan to produce the *Gangnido [Kangnido]*."[12]

Though the Chinese source map *shengjiao guangbeitu* mentioned above is no longer in existence and we do not know its date, we do know that it was from 1389 or earlier—because it was also the source map for the 1389 Chinese map *Da Ming hunyi tu,* which also shows both east and west sides of Africa. (Note that 1389 was *before* Zheng He's voyages from 1405 to 1433.) Ships the size of Zheng He's had been a long time in development. Many years prior, China had ships capable of making those surveys.[13]

Bae questioned: "How did the Ming [Chinese], which maintained a no-maritime-contact policy, learn about other continents such as Europe and Africa?"[14] In asking that, Bae ignored the fact that until 1433 Chinese ships, both private and government owned, were sailing the seas of the world. Long before then the Chinese had developed enormous ships—the size of some of our current ocean liners.

Some believe that the *Ch'onhado* descended from the 1402 *Kangnido* and the 1602 Ricci map. I believe the reverse—that the Africa on the *Kangnido* may have descended from the Africa shown on the *Ch'onhado*. It was not until I had viewed the 1402 *Kangnido* and its Africa that I began to understand and get perspective on the *Ch'onhado*. For me, it is difficult to comprehend (especially with all the contrary evidence) that a primitive map *(Ch'onhado)* would have evolved from more modern ones (*Kangnido* and Ricci). Besides, as we have stated, there is a 1562 Chinese copy of the *Ch'onhado (Tian Xia)* style map that obviously predates the 1602 Ricci map.

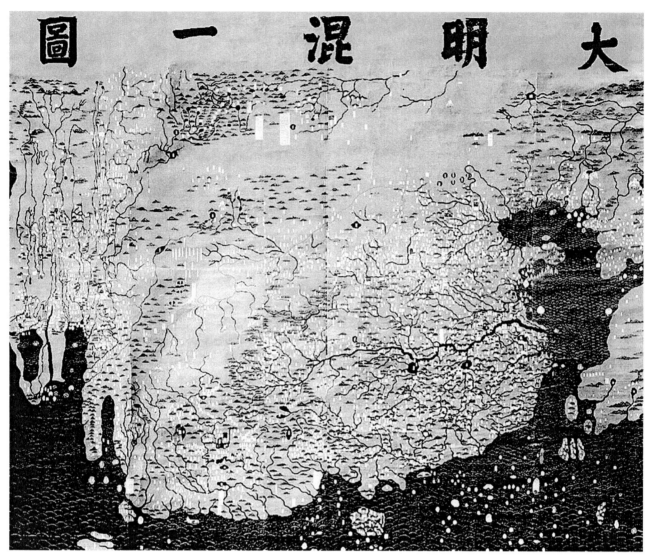

Da Ming Hun Yi Tu above is the 1389 Chinese map from which the 1402 Kangnido was derived. This map is believed to have originated from an even earlier Chinese map. Compare Africa on this map to *Kangnido* and *Tian Xia*.

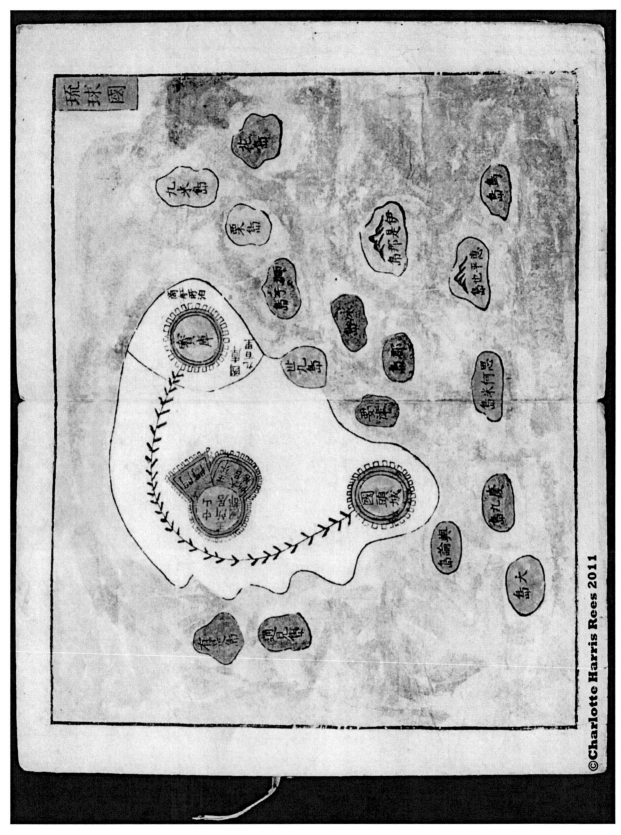

Map of Ryukyu from the *Harris Map Collection*
(Top of map is to the left.)

Map of Ryukyu (Okinawa) in *Ch'onhado* Atlases

Each atlas in which a *Ch'onhado* is found usually also contains various other maps. However, the number of maps and which ones are included varies from atlas to atlas. In some of the older atlases a 1471 version of the *Map of Ryukyu* was included, though use of this style map was discontinued after 1521.

This style *Map of Ryukyu* was used only betwen 1471 and 1521.

This map is derived from *Haedong jegukgi* compiled by Korean Sin Suk-chu in 1471.[15] Bae's statement regarding the *Map of Ryukyu* implies Japanese origin. Bae stated that it:

> appears to be a sailing map . . . . Maritime distances from Japan are written on the map and names of islands near the main island of Japan are recorded in their contemporary Japanese phoneticization of Chinese letters . . . . This indicates that the "Map of Ryukyu" in *Haedong jegukgi* was faithful to the source map.[16]

Direct contact between Korea and Ryukyu was officially discontinued fifty years after the release of *Haedong jegukgi*. After 1521, very different versions of maps of Ryukyu were used. Bae stated that, "Around the end of direct relations with Ryukyu, new types of Ryukyu maps were circulated in Joseon [Korea]." [17]

Based on the above, the *Map of Ryukyu* in *Haedong jegukgi* was used only from 1471 to 1521. However, this map is shown in three of the seven *Harris Map Books*.

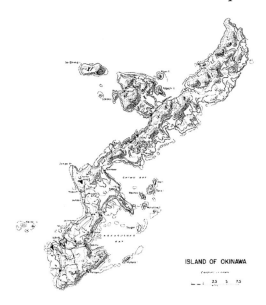

Ryukyu (Okinawa) as shown today.

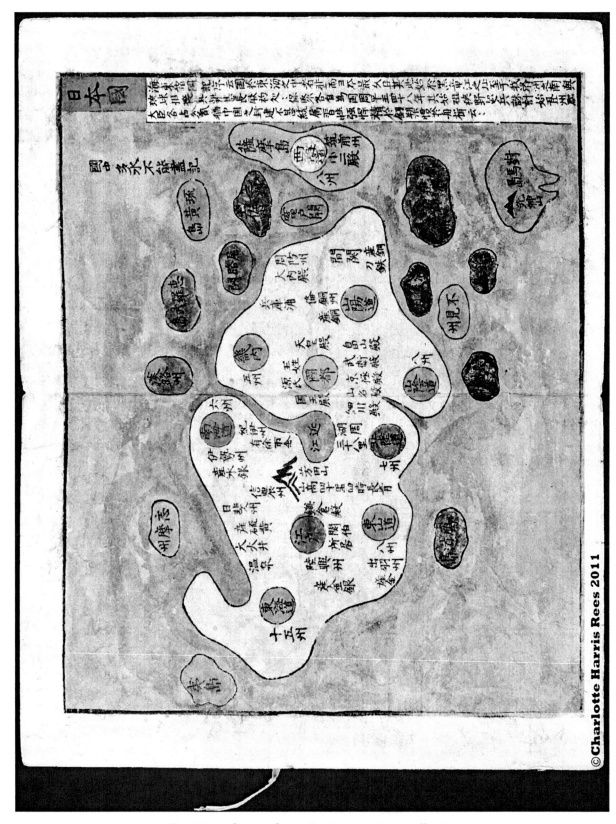

The *Map of Japan* from the *Harris Map Collection*
(Top of map is to the left.)

The *Map of Japan (Ilbon kukto)* Found in the *Ch'onhado* Atlases

McCune stated that, like Ryukyu, the map of Japan shown in this type of atlas was also derived from *Haedong jegukgi,* compiled by Korean Sin Suk-chu in 1471.[18] According to *The History of Cartography,* the earliest known maps of Japan to be printed anywhere are from *Haedong jegukgi,* which was made up of six maps relating to Japan and Korea.[19]

Japanese information was used to make the maps in *Haedong jegukgi.* Note our comments above regarding the Japanese influence on the map of *Map of Ryukyu.* The notes in *Haedong jegukgi* state that routes shown on the map of Japan in that text used Japanese li—each equivalent to ten Korean li.[20]

Sin, who compiled *Haedong jegukgi,* served on a diplomatic mission to Japan in 1443. Ledyard stated: "Later . . . he [Sin] supervised all of Korea's foreign relations for over a decade. The *Haedong Cheguk Ki [Haedong jegukgi]* was a compendium of Japanese and Ryukyu history, geography, and customs, together with a digest of events, precedents, and protocol related to Korea's relations with the two countries."[21]

Reportedly there were hand drawn maps of Japan starting in the ninth century. Writings from the earliest eras indicate that Japan was thought to be elongated from east to west rather than predominantly north to south as it is now displayed.[22]

Perhaps the earliest map of Japan still in existence is the hand drawn one dated 1306 owned by the Ninna Temple in Kyoto. It is damaged, so one cannot view the whole country. That map has notes on it stating that "the map should not be shown to outsiders."[23] Apparently Sin, just a few years later, was able to persuade the Japanese to share information.

Maps of Japan are shown in *Harris Map Books 2, 3, 5,* and *6* and all are the older *Haedong jegukgi* style which run east to west. The maps of Japan in this style in the *Harris Map Books* could be among some of the earliest complete maps of Japan still in existence.

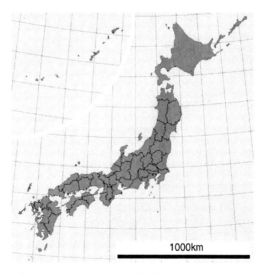

Japan as currently displayed on maps.

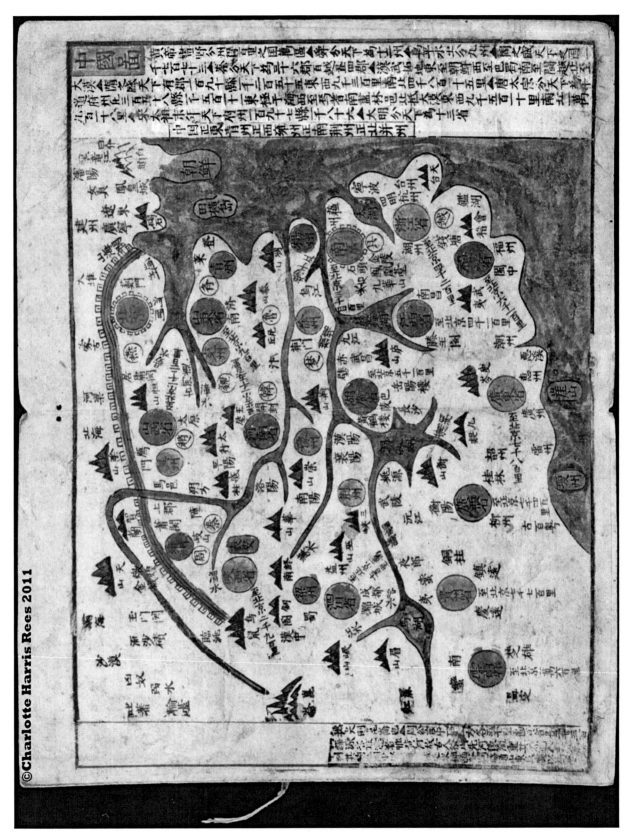

Map of China from the *Harris Map Collection*
(Top of map is to the left.)

The *Map of China (Chungguk-do)* Shown in the *Ch'onhado* Atlases

The map of China shown in the *Harris Map Collection* atlases depicts the Ming provincial arrangement. The Ming Dynasty lasted from 1368 through 1644. The large circles indicate those Ming provinces. The rectangles show the "Nine Isle-lands" (Jiu Zhou) marked out by Yu (ruler of China's first dynasty—approximately 2000 BC) when he drained the floods. The smaller circles mark the major states of the Spring and Autumn period (722-481 BC). The map gives no reference to the Ch'ing Dynasty,[24] which started in AD 1644. It references only what was before.

Smith noted that "the Great Wall might appear in Chinese maps even if they depicted times when the structure did not actually exist."[25] Of course, the Great Wall, which was built in the third century BC, did exist at the time these map atlases were circulating in Korea and is depicted on each of the maps of China in the *Harris Map Collection*.

Maps of China have been around since very early dates. *Old Maps in Japan* shows a detailed map of China from prior to 480 BC.[26] Another Chinese map from AD 1136, *Yuji Tu (Map of the Tracks of Yu),* is modern looking and accurate. It was made using a grid with each square representing 100 li.[27]

There were Korean maps of China starting at least by the 14th century.[28] After the start of the Ch'ing Dynasty, Koreans continued making their own maps of China still showing it as Ming. The Koreans did not accept the Ch'ing, run by the Manchus, as a legitimate Chinese dynasty so kept using the Ming maps. Ledyard wrote that "every published [Korean] map [of China] I have seen from traditional times shows the Ming organization."[29]

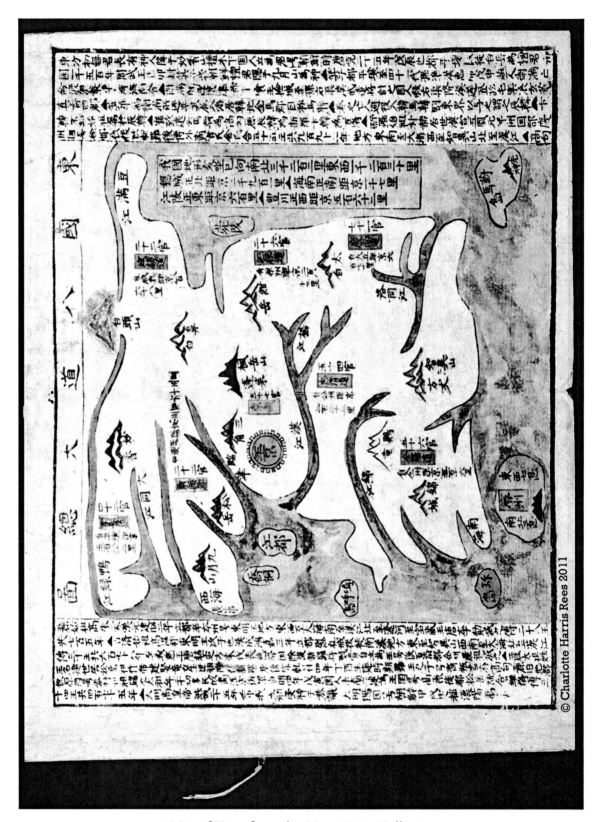

Map of Korea from the *Harris Map Collection*
(Top of map is to the left.)

The *Map of Korea* (*Tongguk-P'alto Taech'ong-do*) in the *Ch'onhado* Atlases

In AD 1018 Korea restructured from having twelve provinces to eight.[30] The *Choson p'alto to* (*Map of Eight Provinces of Korea*) by Yi Hoe was presented to the Korean king in May 1402.[31] It is believed that Korea as depicted on the 1402 *Kangnido,* which came out later that year, was based on that map.

The Geographical Description of the Eight Provinces (P'alto chiri chi) was compiled in 1432. It included not only topographical features but also listed other information including locations of fortifications, roads, mail stations, and garrisons. Later editions in 1481 and 1531 included even more information, including poetry. A 1757 map of Korea, *Tong'yo Ch'ongdo,* shown in *History of Cartography,*[32] is even more accurate and modern.

Dates of the maps suggest *Ch'onhado* atlases were from before Columbus.

However, the maps of Korea in *Ch'onhado* atlases are from the Korean geographical encyclopedia, the *Tongguk Yoji Sungnam,* which is the 1481 version.[33] Because of this 1481 map of Korea in these atlases and also the 1471 versions of maps of Japan and Okinawa, McCune stated: "It may be deduced that the *Chonha Do* was drawn by some Korean scholar-cartographer *two or three decades before 1500* [emphasis mine]."[34]

McCune may be correct in assuming the date when these atlases were first used in Korea and that the *Ch'onhado* had to be in existence to be included. However, this does not address the origin date of the *Ch'onhado* as an individual map.

McCune regarded most of the countries on the *Ch'onhado* as fictitious, so he surely did not mean to suggest pre-Columbian Asian contact with the Americas. However, McCune's dating of the atlases, coupled with the fact that many now recognize the *Ch'onhado* as a real world map that shows the Americas, promotes acceptance of the theory of pre-Columbian arrival of Asians to the Americas.

The Eight Maps of the Korean Provinces in the *Ch'onhado* Atlases

Information on the provincial maps in these atlases helps to date each book. Certain cities appeared or changed names at different dates and, therefore, give clues as to the age of each atlas. It appears that the Koreans attempted to have the provincial maps current when each atlas was assembled. Information on the Korean provinces in these old atlases is very valuable to the Koreans in studying their history. Many of their *Ch'onhado* atlases disappeared during times of war.

63

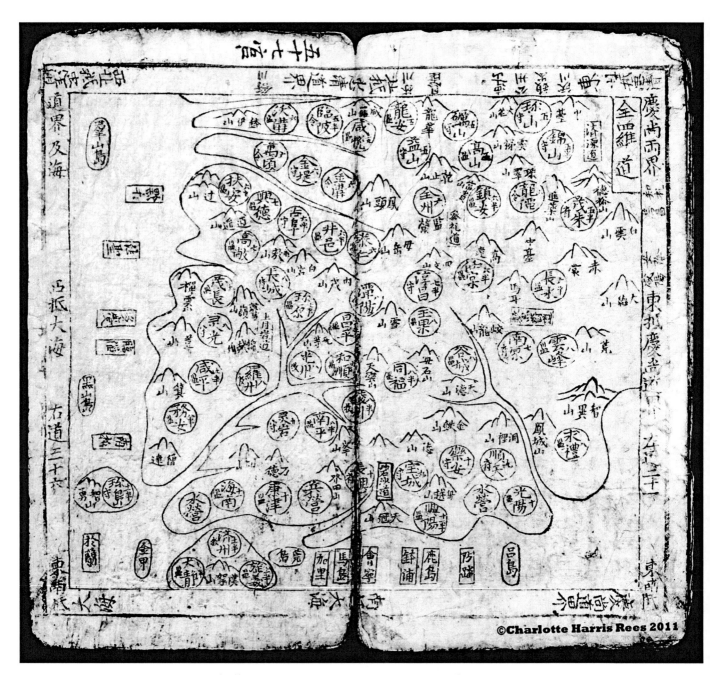

Cholla Province, Korea – *Harris Map Book 7*

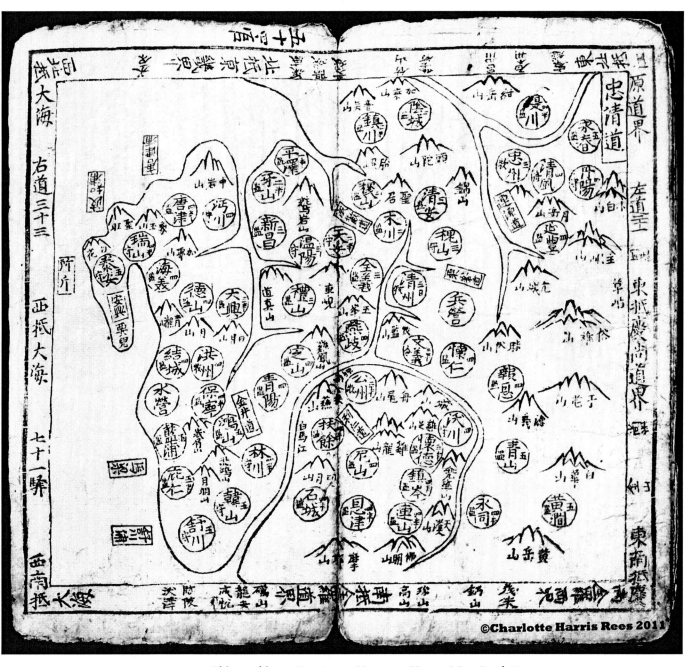

Ch'ungch'ong Province, Korea – *Harris Map Book 7*

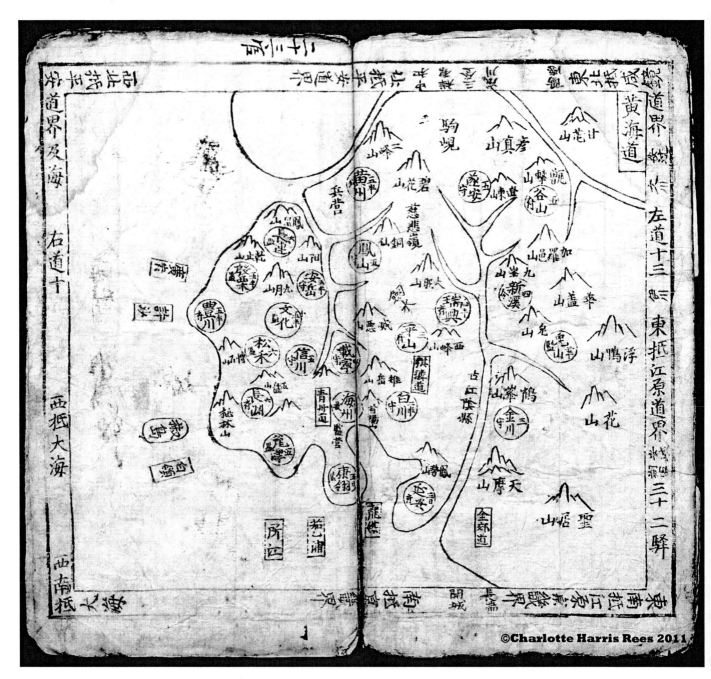

Hwanghae Province, Korea – *Harris Map Book 7*

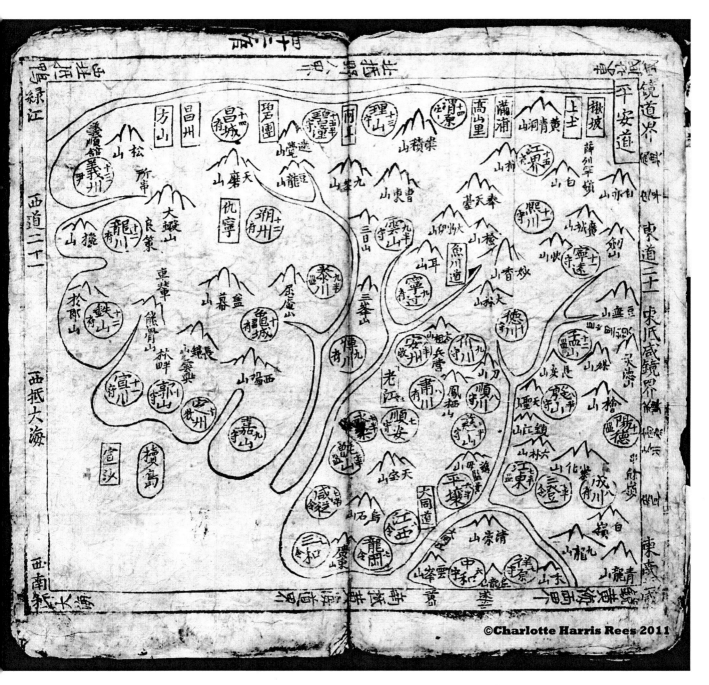

P'yongan Province, Korea – *Harris Map Book 7*

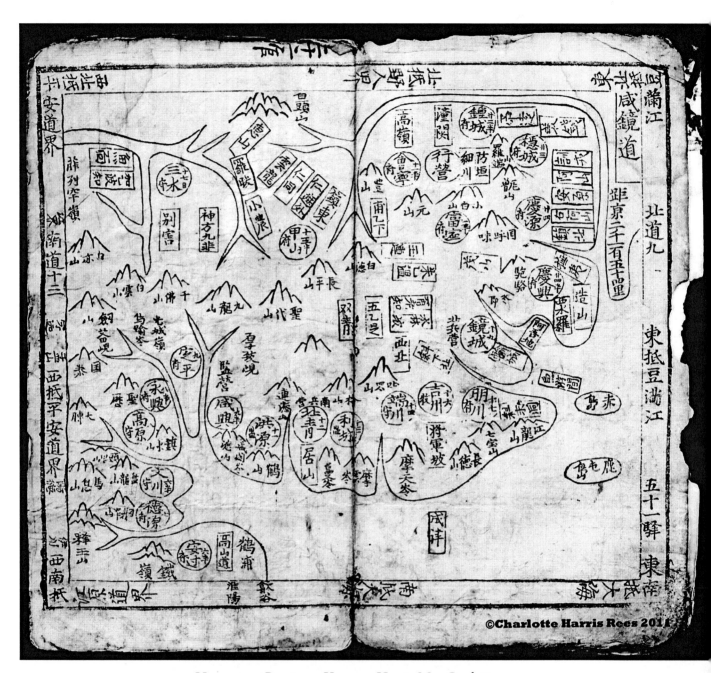

Hamgyong Province, Korea – *Harris Map Book 7*

Kangwon Province, Korea – *Harris Map Book 7*

69

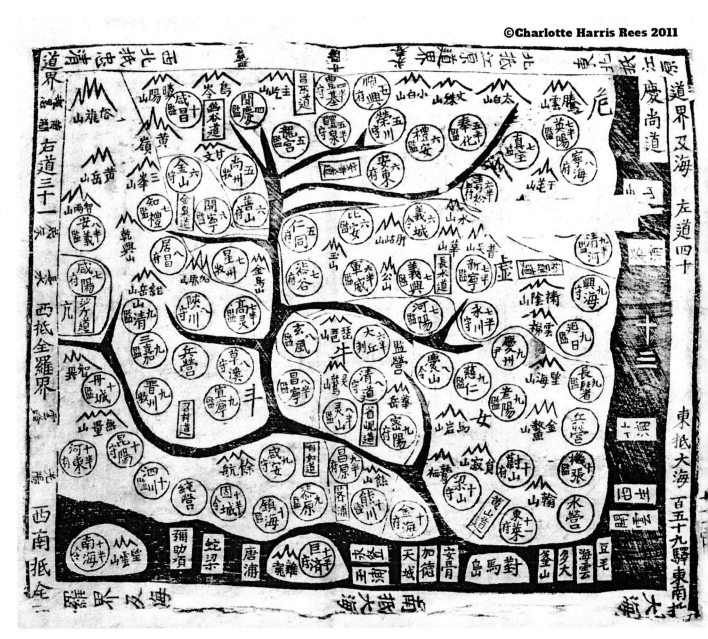

Kyongsang Province, Korea – *Harris Map Book 1*

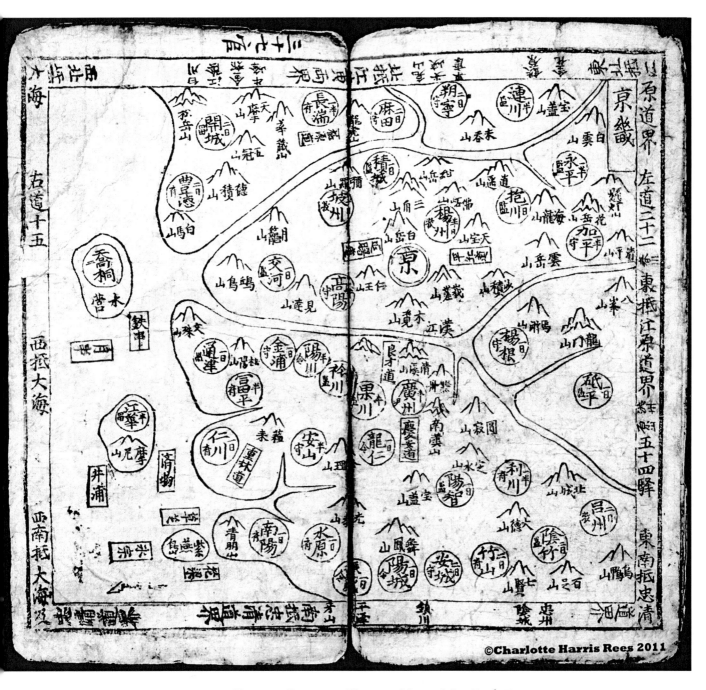

Kyonggi Province, Korea – *Harris Map Book 7*

Clues on Other Korean Maps

Han wrote about another old Korean map, *Han'guk pon yojido (Korean Terrestrial Map)*, undated and now at the National Library of France. According to Han, French soldiers may have taken it as plunder during the Korean "Foreign Disturbance of 1866." That map has an interesting postscript at the bottom:

> A copy of the *Ch'onha yojido (Terrestrial Map of All Under Heaven)* was handed down in our country from the olden days. However, after a period of chaos it disappeared permanently. In recent years a copy of the woodblock-printed world map, made of eight plates and bearing the introduction of Wang Pan, a scholar from Shanyin (modern Shaoxing), was imported from China.
>
> The Heavenly Dynasty (i.e., the Ming) not only regards our country as its closest tributary state but also bestows the favors of rain and dew upon us. Our two countries also share the same standards for ships and carriages. However, since we are unable to see this great kingdom with our own eyes and walk on it with our own feet, making a map of China is most essential.
>
> Now, because this map makes reference to the *Da Ming Guanzhi (Government Structure of the Great Ming)* and the [Da Ming] *Yitongzhi (National Gazetteer of the Great Ming)* it is able to bring together the two capital cities . . . . This shows the magnificence of the Heavenly Court's unification of the world in our times. In addition, information on the lands of Japan, the Ryukyus, and the Nurgan and Huwen regions are included. Future generations shall now know the origin of this map.[35]

This statement is interesting in that it shows Koreans acquiring a world map from China and also that the map included information on Japan and the Ryukyus as the *Ch'onhado* atlases do. Han pointed out that according to the *Chungjong Sillok (Veritable Record of King Chungjong)*, a map titled *Ch'onha yojido* (a generic term for world maps) was presented to the Korean king in 1511 and a map of China in 1519. These maps had been purchased from the Chinese, but lacked detail, so in 1536 the king ordered another world map.

Han stated that in 1537 the king:

> entertained a Ming envoy . . . and on that occasion asked his guest to lend him the *world map* [emphasis mine] he had brought with him. The Chinese envoy replied that he would send him a copy of the map through a Korean envoy when he returned to China. Whether or not his promise was kept is unknown.[36]

These mentions of Koreans getting world maps from China could indicate the source of the *Ch'onhado*.

European Maps of Americas that Show Too Much of America Too Soon

One might wonder what 16th century maps of the Americas might possibly have to do with Asian map books of that era. The problem is that the European maps correctly showed parts of the Americas before they had been explored by Europeans. That the *Waldseemuller* of 1507 shows the West Coast of the Americas separated from Asia might be understandable as an educated guess.

> ## Early European maps correctly showed parts of North America not yet explored by Europeans.

However, in 1566 Bolognino Zaltieri published one of the first European maps of North America to show the Strait of Anian (which today we know as the Bering Strait) separating Asia and North America.[37]

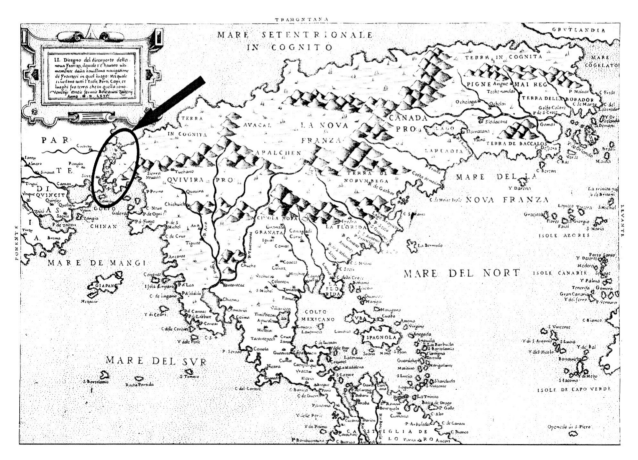

Zaltieri 1566 (circle and arrow pointing to Strait of Anian was inserted by author)

73

In *No Longer on the Map,* Raymond Ramsey indicated that all important cartographers from the 1560s until mid-seventeenth century showed the Strait of Anian.[38] "In the 18th Century the Spanish, Russians and British were all still exploring the West Coast [of North America]. Finally in the late 18th Century the British Parliament offered 20,000 pounds for the discovery for the Strait of Anian, which Captain James Cook accomplished in 1778."[39]

My father wrote in *The Asiatic Fathers of America* that *Tian Xia* maps show Da Han near where today we place Alaska. He believed that the name Anian was derived from Da Han (sometimes spelled Ta Han). *New Records of the Tang Dynasty* indicates that people from Ta Han presented horses and sables skins to China's imperial court during the period AD 627 to 656.

In 2011 in Alaska near the Bering Strait archeologists unearthed a piece of a bronze ring believed to be a horse buckle. A strip of leather attached to that was carbon dated to roughly AD 600 – the same era as the Chinese report above. The finding of bronze in Alaska is puzzling because Alaska never had a bronze age. However, China did.

All those maps were drawn before any Europeans or Americans had ever been to the Strait of Anian. How did they know that the Strait of Anian was there before they found it? Several authors have discussed this phenomenon. The only logical explanation is that Zaltieri and the others had used Asian source maps.

At some point in history, the Chinese drew pictures of what they thought the fantastic creatures mentioned in the *Shan Hai Jing* should look like. Bagrow demonstrates in *History of Cartography* that nearly identical drawings are shown in the AD 1493 *Nuremberg Chronicle*.[40]

Anatole Andro, author of *The 1421 Heresy,* shows that these creatures in the *Nuremberg Chronicle* were depicted in this text by German physician Hartmann Schedel as "people of the Great Kahn."[41] This "Great Kahn" designation clearly indicates that the information came from Asia. Therefore, since that by at least 1493 Europeans had illustrations from the Chinese geography the *Shan Hai Jing,* they most likely also had the *Shan Hai Jing* itself plus other information including Chinese maps and navigational charts.

Lam Yee Din wrote that the 1565 *Forlani Map of the Known World* shown in *Cartographia: Mapping Civilizations*[42] also has the 91 degree Chinese orientation that we discussed regarding the 1602 Ricci map. This could be further indication that early European world maps were based on Chinese source maps.

Chapter 7
Harris Map Books

The seven map books in the Harris Collection

The first Harris atlas was found in Korea. It has been stated by reliable experts that all the *Harris Map Books* are Korean, that most of the maps in each book are of Korean provinces, and that these are genuine *Ch'onhado* maps. They were viewed at the Library of Congress by, among other experts, Dr. Xiaocong Li, Professor of Historical Geography and Cartography, Peking University, Beijing, and by Dr. Gari Ledyard, Professor Emeritus, Columbia University, who is also a leading expert on maps of this style. Li and Ledyard each gave verbal analysis.

Though they are in Korean books, the *Harris Maps* are all in Chinese characters. Perhaps these were at one time government-owned books. After Korean script was in use, Koreans continued to print their important government texts in Chinese.

The *Harris Maps* are on white mulberry bark paper. Once after hearing this, a schoolgirl asked me whether they were on strips of mulberry bark. It is quite the contrary. Though mulberry bark is used in the process, the product these maps are on is a fine specimen of paper. The *Harris Maps* were printed from carved wooden blocks.

In typical Asian tradition, the front of each *Harris Map Book* starts with the right cover—what Caucasians would consider the back of the book. The world map is shown first, followed by the other maps.

The numbering of the *Harris Map Books* has no special significance. *Harris Map Book 5* was the first map found by my father, Dr. Hendon Harris, Jr. We do not know where he purchased the other maps in his collection, but assume that he found them in Asia. One of the *Harris Maps* has "18th year of the Ming" (1386) on it. However, we do not know whether this is dating it or describing an event.

The *Harris Map Books* have not been carbon dated. That process is expensive, requires cutting a piece from the document, and does not precisely pinpoint dates. Recently, someone wrote to me about her hand drawn *Ch'onhado* that is not in an atlas. That map looks old, but since there was nothing else in the document (other maps, etc.) with which to have her map dated, she decided to have it carbon dated by a very reputable company. She said that the dating concluded that her map was made sometime between 1695 and 1955. It was a huge disappointment to this woman not to receive a more precise dating. Since most Korean maps of this style were made during that time period, I am sure that anyone who knows even a little about *Ch'onhado* maps could have guessed just as accurately.

Colors on the Maps

A few of the *Harris Maps* were had colors added by hand. *Harris Map Books 5 and 6* are especially noteworthy for their beautiful coloration throughout those atlases. In Japan similar maps for important people had color added by hand.

Archaic Characters on Some of the Maps

I recently learned that the character for country (guo) in the name for China (Zhongguo) on *Harris World Map 5* and some of the other Harris world maps shown above is a style that was used only during the Tang Dynasty (AD 618-907).

I believe that during the time my father, Dr. Hendon Harris, Jr., was writing *The Asiatic Fathers of America* in 1972 and 1973, that he had only what we now designate as *Harris Map 5*. He described his map as having red seals. He mentioned on that map an archaic word that would have been written differently after the start of the Sui Dynasty in AD 581. I also see that form of the character on some of the other *Harris World Maps 2, 6,* and *7*.

In English, we no longer use the word "ye" for "you." Chinese over their long history have also changed how they wrote words. Father believed that the way the word was shown on the map indicated it came from a prior period.

Chinese written words are made up of multiple pictographs called radicals. In this particular character (word), part of it is what looks like a tree without leaves. Before AD 581 the "tree" radical appeared on the left side of the character. After that date it appeared on the right. The tree also appears to the left on some of his other world maps. My father wrote:

> Professor Charles Feng and Rev. Stephen Wu examined the dictionary of ancient Chinese words and discovered that this form of the word [with the tree to the left] first occurred in the Han Dynasty [202 BC-AD 9], and was the common style until the Sui Dynasty [581-618] after which time the . . . [tree] appears on the other side . . . This word is . . . strong evidence that the Harris map . . . contains information from the pre-Christian era.[1]

Harris wrote that this could be found in northern Mexico on *Harris World Map 5*. To view this character, look at the far right side of that map and follow down that coast to near the bottom. Look for the mountains just below an inlet on the right side. The word is the character at the far right side of that caption. The title is "Su-Door Mountains." Harris wrote: "This is the same word that is used in the name of the Chinese province Kiangsu . . . . The same word appears in Suchow. Furthermore, it has exactly the same sound as the "su" of the Sioux Indians . . . who have been scientifically tested and shown to have Asiatic blood!"[2]

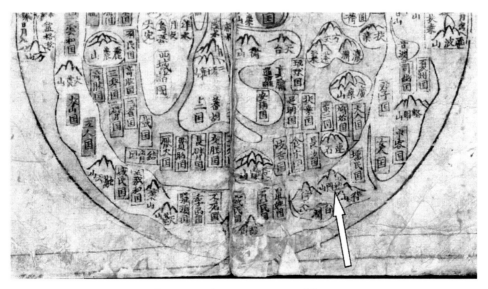

Archaic word on *Harris World Map 5*

What does this imply that characters from different dynasties were used on this same old map? It suggests that the original of this map was first drawn long ago. Perhaps the printing block for this map was carved during the early Tang Dynasty and the artist faithfully copied words as they were written in previous editions of the map.

Several Chinese dynasties lasted hundreds of years. However, it was only 37 years between the start of the Sui Dynasty (AD 581) to the start of the Tang (618). It is conceivable that the artist was alive during all three dynasties mentioned above and just carried his word usage forward. For some reason Nakamura also contended that maps of this style originated before the Tang Dynasty.

Map Folds

One of the items of interest in the *Harris Map Books* is the way that the individual maps unfold. *Harris Map Book 5* unfolds as a timeline does to a length of over eleven feet (342 cm). There are maps on one side and large stylized calligraphy characters on the other.

Harris Map Book 4 is only about the size of a checkbook. Each page is connected to the cover but separately unfolds to full size. Each page has to be folded back before proceeding to the next page. *Harris Map 6* has two starting places so one can start at either the front or back of the book and see a different series of maps.

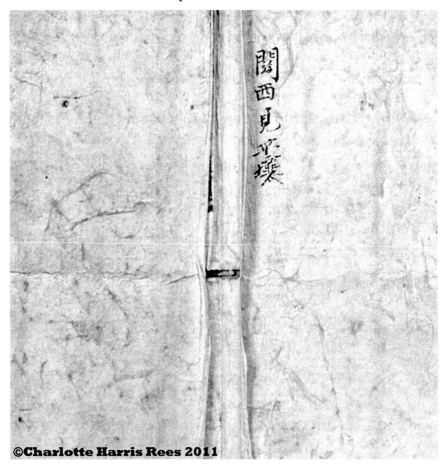

Unusual map folds in *Harris Map Book 4*
(Love note is on far left of bottom photo.)

Book Titles

It has been noted that the titles of *Harris Map Books* 4, 5, and 6 are different from the others. We do not know the significance of this.

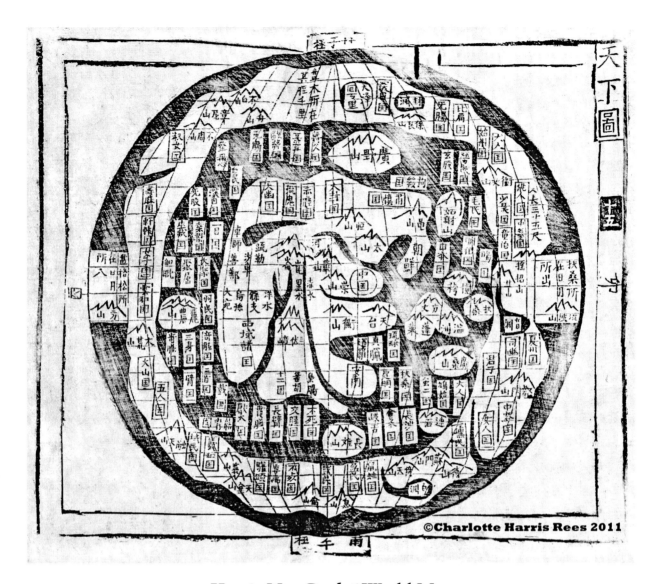

Harris Map Book 1 World Map

There are eleven maps in this book: a world map, maps of Korea and China, and maps of the eight Korean provinces. There are no colored markings on the maps in this atlas.

Dating: The printing block for the last page in the book was most likely carved between 1787 and 1823. Chingjin shows on the last page. P'ungdok, which was absorbed into Kaesson in 1823, is still on the map. The blocks were in good shape when this was printed.

One expert stated that since the world map in this book has false graticule (false latitude and longitude lines), it would suggest that the book was probably assembled **in the late 1890s**. Korean Young Ki Lee put the date in the **late 18th century**.

The History of Cartography shows a *Ch'onhado* map owned by the Library of Congress that was printed from the same block as the *Ch'onhado* in this atlas. There is also a similar map, owned by Lee Chan, shown on page 194 of *Old Maps of Korea*. The *Harris Map Book 1* world map appears to be in better condition than either of those maps.

On the eight Korean Do (provinces) are numbers in the sea that are thought to be the names of twenty-eight star constellations, which was the way ancient Chinese mapped the night sky. See reference to these charts with 28 spokes in *Did Ancient Chinese Explore America*.

Analysis Done by Young Ki Lee in 2005

<u>Map Book #1</u>

Cover title: No cover title

Caption title: *Ch'onha-do*

Printing: Wood Block, no color

Probable Date: Late 18th century

Atlas size: 34 cm x 41 cm

Map size: 27.5 cm x 33.5 cm

Material: Mulberry bark paper, tied with two strings on the left side

Number of Place Names

1. Main Continent: 29, including China and Korea
2. Inner Sea Ring: 56, including Japan and Okinawa
3. Outer Land Ring: 53, with three trees
4. Total: 138

Order of Maps

1. *Ch'onha-do (World Map)*
2. *Chungguk-do (Map of China)*
3. *Tongguk P'alto Taech'ong (Map of Korea)*
4. *Kyonggi-do (Map of Kyonggi Province)*
5. *Ch'ungch'ong-do (Map of Ch'ungch'ong Province)*
6. *Cholla-do (Map of Cholla Province)*
7. *Kyongsang-do (Map of Kyongsang Province)*
8. *Hwanghae-do (Map of Hwanghae Province)*
9. *P'yongan-do (Map of P'yongan Province)*
10. *Kangwon-do (Map of Kangwon Province)*
11. *Hamgyong-do (Map of Hamgyong Province)*

Description

1. Lee Chan's collection and Yongnam University have copies printed from the same block. See page 156 of Lee Chan, *Han'guk ui Ko chido*, 1st ed. Seoul: Pomusa, 1991. Copy of Lee Chan's collection includes map of Japan and map of Okinawa.

2. The edge of each page has a number.

3. Under the caption title, there is the number 15.

4. Sino-Korean character numbers (could be pagination) in white in the water areas on each map:

   Map of China (3), *Map of Korea* (6), *Map of Hamgyong Province* (7), *Map of P'yongan Province* (8), *Map of Hwanghae Province* (9), *Map of Kangwon Province* (10), *Map of Kyonggi Province* (11), *Map of Ch'ungch'ong Province* (12), *Map of Kyongsang Province* (13), *Map of Cholla Province* (14).

5. Each provincial map has the number of jurisdictions in handwriting (This information could be a good clue to judge the probable date.)

Kyonggi Province:	33
Ch'ungch'ong Province:	54
Cholla Province:	57
Kyongsang Province:	71
Hwanghae Province:	23
P'yongan Province:	42
Kangwon Province:	26
Hamgyong Province:	24

6. The world map has false latitude and longitude lines.

7. The world map has compass directions on each side (North, South, East, West).

8. Made from same wood block as map #3? (See map of Ch'ungch'ong Province, same repair mark on the left upper side.).

9. Printed on both sides: Double leaves in oriental style.

10. Perhaps the cover is missing: there is evidence of double leaves on world map with one side missing.

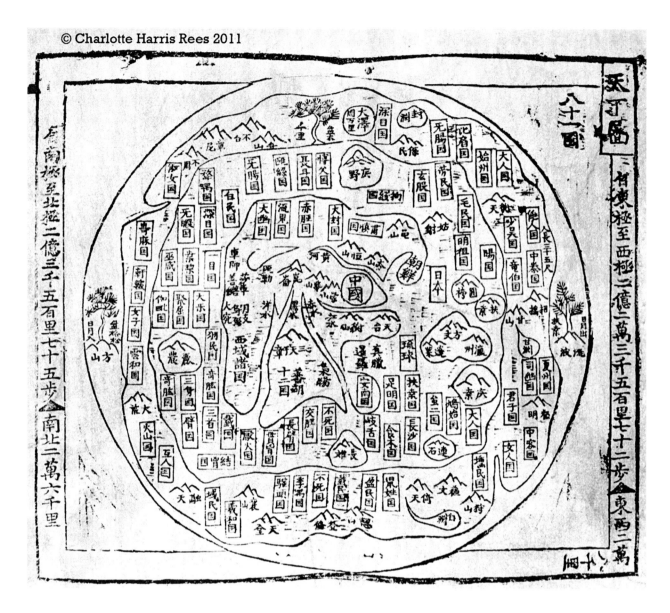

Harris Map Book 2 World Map

There are thirteen maps in this set: a world map, separate maps of Korea, Japan, Okinawa, and China, and maps of the eight Korean provinces. No colors have been added to the maps in this book.

Dating: The map of Okinawa in this atlas is a style produced in 1471 and replaced around 1521. (See explanation under *Harris Map Book 3*.)

One expert thought that the paper seems to be more modern than that of any other map in the collection. Because of that, he put the dating of this map at around the **1920s**. However, others thought that date too recent since Japan occupied Korea in 1920, and did not believe maps like this would have been made during that period. Another expert who viewed the map thought it **18th to 19th century**. Young Ki Lee thought **mid-18th century**.

This map book was printed on paper with a gray background. The front surface of the paper appears to have been washed with a gray tinting while the back retains the natural off-white color. The size of the pages is not exactly uniform. The pages are stitched together to form a book without a cover.

Analysis Done by Young Ki Lee in 2005

<u>Map Book #2</u>

Cover title: No cover title
Caption title: *Ch'onhado*
Printing: Wood Block, no color
Probable Date: Mid-18th century
Atlas size: 31.5 cm x 42 cm
Map size 26.5 cm x 31.5 cm

Number of Place Names

1. Main Continent: 31, including China and Korea
2. Inner Sea Ring: 56, including Japan and Okinawa
3. Outer Land Ring: 52, with three trees
4. Total: 139

Order of Maps:

1. *Ch'onhado-do (World map)*
2. *Chungguk-do (Map of China)*
3. *Tongguk P'alto Taech'ongdo (Map of Korea)*
4. *Kyonggi-do (Map of Kyonggi Province)*
5. *Hwanghae-do (Map of Hwanghae Province)*
6. *Kangwon-do (Map of Kangwon Province)*
7. *Cholla-do (Map of Cholla Province)*
8. *Ch'ungch'ong-do (Map of Ch'ungch'ong Province)*
9. *Kyongsang-do (Map of Kyongsang Province)*
10. *P'yongan-do (Map of P'yongan Province)*
11. *Hamgyong-do (Map of Hamgyong Province)*
12. *Ilbonguk (Map of Japan)*
13. *Yuguguk (Map of Okinawa)*

Description

1. National Library of Korea has similar copy titled "*Yoji koram tobo.*" Please see page 394 of Lee, Chan. *Han'guk ui Ko chido*. 1st ed. Seoul: Pomusa, 1991. Much information and/or description appears in handwriting in the National Library's copy. This Map #2 has information only about the distance between East and West, North and South.

2. "P'alsibil-kuk," which means "eighty-one countries," appears on the left side of the caption title.

3. Right side of the *Ch'onhado* says: "From East Pole to West Pole, it is 200,023,572 steps. From east to west, it is 28,000 li."

4. Left side of *Ch'onhado* says: "From South Pole to North Pole is 200,003,575 steps. From south to north, it is 26,000 li."

5. The *Map of China* does not show Japan and Okinawa.

6. Each paper has some kind of symbol (looks like '+') on the top center position.

7. The National Library of Korea's copy used same wood block, dated mid-18th century. It is almost impossible, I think, for that woodblock to survive until 1920.

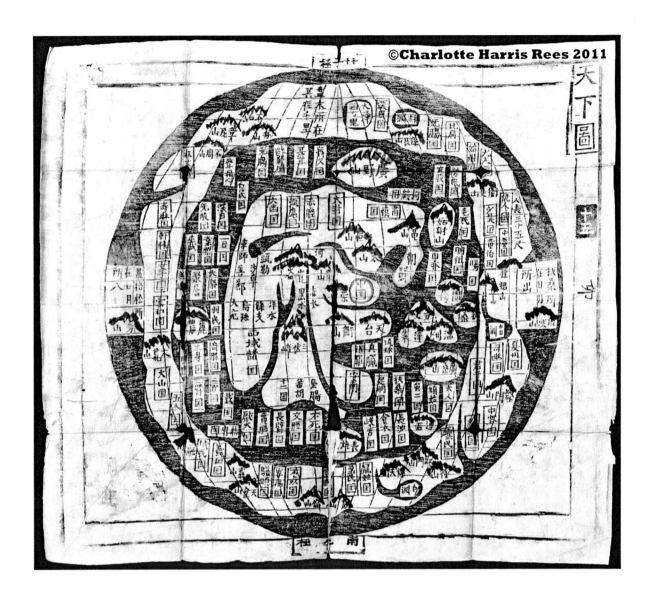

Harris Map Book 3 World Map

There are thirteen maps in this set: a world map, maps of Korea, Japan, China, and Okinawa, and maps of the eight Korean provinces.

Dating: In *Korea Journal*, Spring 2008, Bae Woo Sung shows an identical map of Ryukyu (Okinawa) as in this atlas. Bae states that this map, found in *Haedong Jegukgi*, was used only between 1471 and around 1521 and that it appeared to be a sailing map.[3] Maritime distances from Japan are shown on it. Fifty years after the release of this map, direct contact between Korea and Okinawa was officially discontinued. After 1521, Korean maps of Okinawa looked very different. They no longer included the sailing information and instead showed a layout of the royal capital. This map in *Harris Map Book 3* is also very similar to the depiction of Okinawa as shown in *Harris Map Books* 2 and 6.

The wooden blocks for the Korean provinces were carved at different dates. On the page depicting P'yongan Province in *Harris Map Book 3*, Re San is shown. Re San was reorganized and renamed Ch'osan in 1776. Therefore, this block was carved or was based on a source earlier than 1776. The map of Hamgyong Province shows Changjin, which was created in 1787. This block therefore was carved later. Some believe that the latitude and longitude lines on this *Ch'onhado* indicates that the album as a whole was assembled in the **1890s**, even though earlier block prints may have been used for some of the maps.

The world map appears to be from the same printing block as that in *Harris Map Book 1*, except in *Harris Map Book 3* the tops of mountain ranges are enhanced with blue coloring. Below the title *Tian Xia* is the number "15." This may be page 15 or the 15th edition. The character below that is "East." The top of the map shows the North Pole and the bottom the South Pole. The world map has a superimposed "false graticule" that one expert thought could indicate that it was printed in the 1890s. Another expert put the date at **18th century**. Young Ki Lee chose **late 18th century**.

According to Dr. Gari Ledyard, who viewed the collection in October 2003 while it was at the Library of Congress, the sheets are a double thickness of "rice paper." This is actually another name for thin layers any of several different types of oriental paper, including mulberry bark paper.

There is no book cover and the maps are loose, not bound into an album. Based on creases in the maps, they may have at one time been folded like the maps in *Harris Map Book 4*. The maps are in very fragile condition and there is writing on the back sides of the maps—perhaps an inventory. Paper was scarce and perhaps they were produced from recycled paper.

There are 28 constellations shown in the eight Korean Do maps.

Analysis Done by Young Ki Lee in 2005

Map Book #3

Cover title: No Cover Title

Caption title: *Ch'onha-do*

Printing: Wood Block, hand coloring (Blue, Red)

Probable Date: Late 18th century

Atlas size: 15 cm x 9 cm when folded

Map size: 30.5 cm x 35.5 cm

Material: Mulberry bark paper

Number of Place Names

1. Main Continent: 31, including China and Korea
2. Inner Sea Ring: 56, including Japan and Okinawa

3. Outer Land Ring: 52, with three trees
4. Total: 139
5. This *Ch'onhado* does not have three symbolic trees; only the names of the trees are shown.

Contents of atlas: (Maps are loose pages not bound into an album)

1. *Ch'onha-do* (*World Map*)
2. *Chungguk-do* (*Map of China*)
3. *Tongguk P'alto Taech'ong* (*Map of Korea*)
4. *Kyonggi-do* (*Map of Kyonggi Province*)
5. *Ch'ungch'ong-do* (*Map of Ch'ungch'ong Province*)
6. *Cholla-do* (*Map of Cholla Province*)
7. *Kyongsang-do* (*Map of Kyongsang Province*)
8. *Hwanghae-do* (*Map of Hwanghae Province*)
9. *P'yongan-do* (*Map of P'yongan Province*)
10. *Kangwon-do* (*Map of Kangwon Province*)
11. *Hamgyong-do* (*Map of Hamgyong Province*)
12. *Ilbon Kukto* (*Map of Japan*)
13. *Yugu Kukto* (*Map of Okinawa*)

Description

1. The world map appears to be printed from the same wood block as Map #1.
2. No cover. Perhaps originally it was a pocket-sized atlas like Map #4. Center portion of each page has some evidence of being torn off from the original.
3. Under the caption title of *Ch'onha-do* is the number 15.
4. Sino-Korean character numbers (could be pagination?) in white in the water areas on each map: *Map of China* (3), *Map of Korea* (6), *Map of Hamgyong Province* (7), *Map of P'yongan Province* (8), *Map of Hwanghae Province* (9), *Map of Kangwon Province* (10), *Map of Kyonggi Province* (11), *Map of Ch'ungch'ong Province* (12), *Map of Kyongsang Province* (13), *Map of Cholla Province* (14), *Map of Japan* (4), *Map of Okinawa* (5)
5. The world map has false latitude and longitude lines.
6. The world map has a compass direction on each side (North, South, East, West) in Chinese characters.
7. The back of the map appears to have been made from used bookkeeping paper.
8. Preservation is strongly recommended.

Harris Map Book 4 World Map

This usually commands the most attention of any map book in the Harris collection. It has unique folds, appears to be very old, and is only about the size of a checkbook.

Dating: This book does not show Changjin, which was created in 1787. Kumch'on, which was replaced by Sihung in 1795, is still in this map book. Therefore, *Harris Map Book 4* was probably produced earlier than 1787.

Old Maps of Korea shows an image of a map from the same block as the world map in *Harris Map Book 4*. That map, owned by Lee Chan, is dated 1684 because it has "Kanghui 23rd year" written on it. The twenty-third year of Kanghui of Ch'ing (China) was 1684. Normally *Ch'onhado* maps were never signed or dated.

One expert believed this particular atlas was from **earlier than 1787**. Another dated this to late Ming—**before 1644—probably late 1500s**. Young Ki Lee, not knowing what the others had said, dated it **1684 (?)**.

This small pocket-sized map book has a dark brown covering. Experts have conjectured that perhaps it was made in this unusually small size for a traveler and was possibly a governor's or district magistrate's reference handbook. Each map page unfolds separately from the other maps. There is no color on the pages. The world map has no grid.

Unusual Names for the Korean Provinces: There are ten maps in this book: a world map, a map of China, and maps of the eight Korean provinces. Interestingly, a map of Korea is not included and the titles for the Korean provinces are not as they are usually listed. The way they are actually listed on the maps is shown in Young Ki Lee's comments below. Why the provincial titles on these maps are different from those in all the other map books needs to be explored.

In Chinese Maps: Images of 'All Under Heaven,' Dr. Richard Smith, though he discusses other *Tian Xia* maps as Korean, presents a map from this block print as a Chinese map.[4]

Love Notes: Kwang On Yoo spent months studying photos of the maps for me. He concluded that almost all of the script is Chinese. However, in the unique folds of P'yongan Province in *Harris Map Book 4*, Yoo discovered love notes in Korean. On the outside of that map is: "My red heart is for Kim Sung," then on the Hwanghae map is, "My red heart is Kim Sung X." The first set contains three Korean characters out of eight.

The second declaration was done in a less grammatically correct manner and with only two Korean letters. Yoo stated that "these are not part of the maps but my guess is one girl wrote on the cover of the map much later. She didn't even have a proper brush to write!" Perhaps the notes were written in the folds of the map for her lover to find as he traveled. There is no indication when the love notes were added.

International Dispute: One fourth of the world map is missing (the left side). Unfortunately, that means that one fourth of the page behind it (Kangwon Do) is also missing. To Koreans this is an important loss in that the missing portion of Kangwon Do is where it embraces Wu San (Dok Do). There is an international dispute between Japan and Korea over ownership of **Dok Do**—a heated one because valuable gas hydrates have been located there. The Korean Ministry calculated that it was enough to meet thirty years of demand for Korea.[5] Dok Do is shown on some of the other *Harris Map* atlases, which establishes that Dok Do was originally part of Korea.

On one of the maps in *Harris Map Book 4*, **Dema Do** (Japanese Tsushima) is located next to the port city of Pusan, clearly showing it was a Korean territorial island even though it was later taken by Japanese in 1866. Thanks to Kwang On Yoo, on 9/26/2008, the Seoul [Korea] Metro (circulation over half a million daily), ran an article with a picture of Dr. Hendon Harris, Jr., and pictures of the covers of *Secret Maps of the Ancient World* and the abridged *The Asiatic Fathers of America*. Also pictured was Dema Do in Gyengsang Do on the *Harris Maps*. The article discussed that Dema Do is shown on the *Harris Maps* as part of Korea.

Yoo reported that in 2005 the South Korea municipal assembly designated June 19 as "Demado Day" and claimed it as South Korean territory. (Demado is the Korean pronunciation of the Chinese characters of Tsushima.) In 2008, fifty members of the South Korean parliament proposed making another demand for Tsushima.

Military Secrets: The most important part of the Korean maps may be the information at the bottom of each province. This map book contains what would have been military secrets at the time: commentary about safe locations for people to hide in the mountains in case of war and sites of water wells. It lists the locations of Korean naval bases and postal routes.

Turtle Ships: A total of twelve renowned Korean turtle ships are shown on four different maps in this atlas. They are shown in Kyongsang Do in the Ports of Dongrae (1), and Tongyong (2). Turtle ships are also shown in Cholla Do (1), Ch'ungch'ong Do (2), and P'yongan Do (6). It is significant that there were twelve ships depicted at one time. Prevailing belief is that Korea had only a few turtle ships at any time. They were used most successfully during a period of war with Japan (1592-1598).

The Maritime Museum in Oxnard, California, has a model replica of the Korean armored turtle ships. When I visited there in 2010, the museum docent told me that the turtle ships were by far the children's favorite exhibit. Not only were the Korean turtle ships armored, but they were also covered with sharp spikes usually hidden under straw. An enemy attempting to board would be impaled.

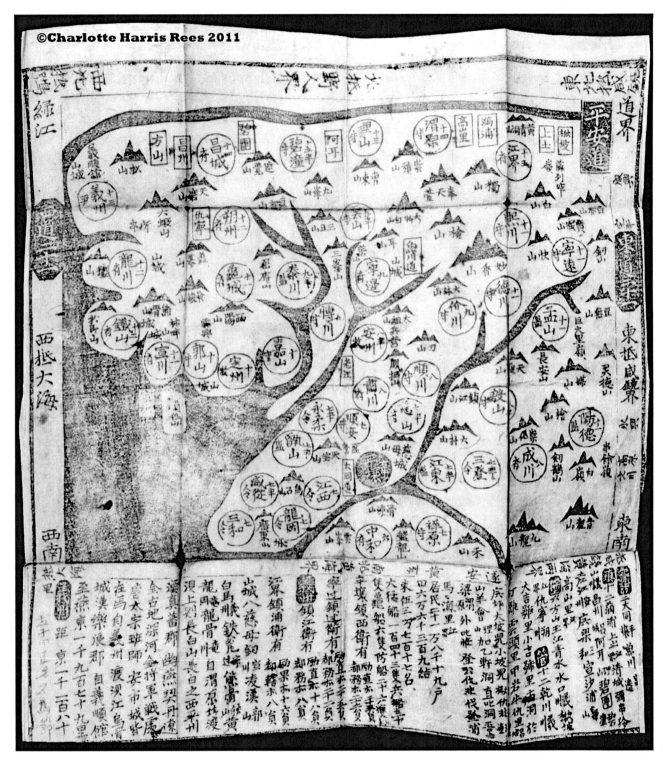

P'yongan Province in *Harris Map Book 4* references 6 turtle ships.

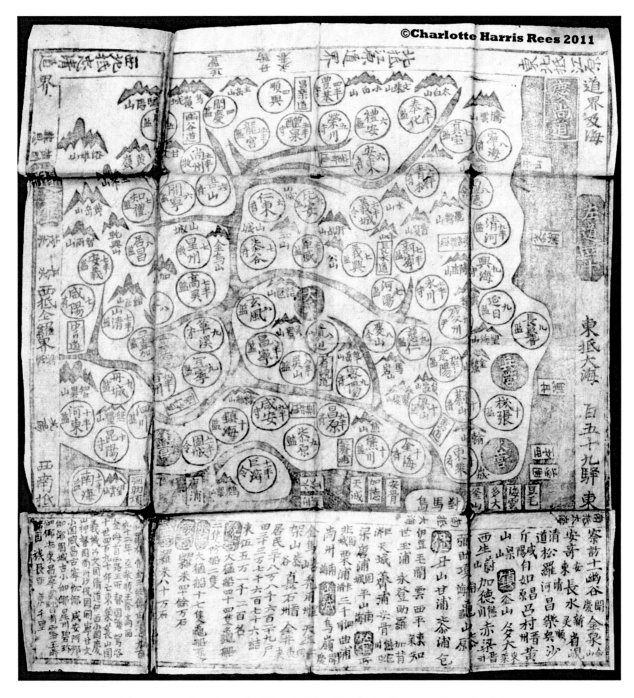

Kyongsang Province in *Harris Map Book 4* references 3 turtle ships.

A man's name is signed on the cover of *Harris Map Book 4*. Yoo commented: "Ledyard stated that one man used to sign the *Ch'onhado* without using his real name. He might be a mapmaker or a collector. Maybe this is the same man he was talking about who wrote his name on this cover."

Harris Map Book 4 indicates that it is 3,000 li across the moon and sun. My father wrote regarding this: "The delightful information in no way blemished the charm and sincerity of their almost desperate effort to be scientifically helpful."

Analysis Done by Young Ki Lee in 2005

Map Book #4

Cover title: *Tungnam*

Caption title: *Ch'onha [Ch'ongdo]* (World Map) (Part of the title is missing.)

Printing: Wood Block, no color

Probable Date: 1684? Atlas size: 17 cm x 9 cm

Map size 32.5 cm x 31 cm

Material: Mulberry bark paper, oiled strengthened paper used in cover

Number of Place Names

1. Main Continent: 31, including China and Korea
2. Inner Sea Ring: cannot count because of missing portion
3. Outer Land Ring: cannot count because of missing portion
4. Total: unknown

Order of Maps

1. *Ch'onha [Ch'ongdo]* (*World map*)
2. *Chungguk* (*Map of China*)
3. *Kijon Kyon Kwangju* (*Map of Kyonggi Province*)
4. *Hoso Kyon Ch'ungju* (*Map of Ch'ungch'ong Province*)
5. *Honam Kyon Kwangju* (*Map of Cholla Province*)
6. *Yongnam Kyon Chinju* (*Map of Kyongsang Province*)
7. *Kwanbuk Kyon Kapsim* (*Map of Hamgyong Province*)
8. *Kwanso Kyon P'yongyang* (*Map of P'yongan Province*)
9. *Haeso Kyon Munhwa* (*Map of Hwanghae Province*)
10. *Kangwon-do* (*Map of Kangwon Province*) part of map is missing

Description

1. Lee Chan's collection has a similar copy. Please see p. 28 of Lee Chan's *Han'guk ui Ko chido*, 1st ed., Seoul: Pomusa, 1991.
2. On *Ch'onha-do* and *Map of Kangwon Province*, a portion is missing.
3. Lee Chan's copy shows important publication date information on left portion of *Ch'onhado*, which is missing in *Harris Map 4*. Lee Chan's copy has "Kanghui 23-yon

Kapja . . ." Kanghui was the 19th King of Choson Dynasty, the period was 1674 thru 1720. So the "Kanghui 23" is 1684.

4. Each province map has handwritten census statistics. (This information could be a good clue to judge the probable date.)

5. The *Ch'onha-do* shows some celestial information on the right side and some distance information on the left side, such as: "Ch'onji chigan sanggo soak icholli," The distance between heaven and earth is 400,002,000 li.

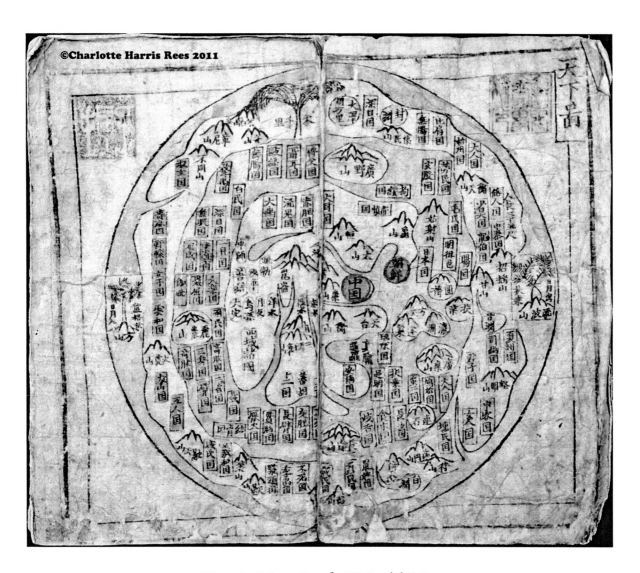

Harris Map Book 5 World Map

This, the first map book found by Dr. Harris, was purchased in Korea in 1972 and contains ten maps: a world map, a map of Japan, and maps of each of the eight Korean provinces. Korea, China, and Okinawa are not included. The large brown cover resembles leather, but is actually a paper product.

Dating: The map block appears to have been carved before 1767 because An'um, which was changed to San'um in 1767, is still on the map. A locality created in 1787 is not on the map either. The paper and book cover appear old. It could have been made **before 1767.** One expert thought that it was from the **Ming Dynasty before 1644 and perhaps from the late 1500s.**

The last three characters of the title of this book are "country map attached," so perhaps it was a county official's reference handbook.

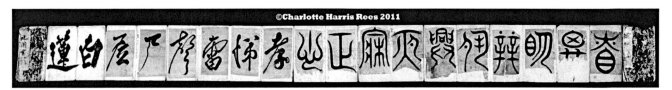

Reverse side of *Harris Map Book 5* unfolded

Harris Map Book 5 unfolds to show a long display of eighteen large, highly stylized Chinese characters on the back. Reading from right to left the last two characters are "White Lotus." The lotus was dear to Buddhists. The characters describe different virtues. The characters and the maps are two separate subjects and have nothing to do with each other. The first two bold characters on this cover translate as "Embroidered Decoration." As there is no embroidery work on the book, surely it refers to the beautifully embellished full-page characters on the back of the maps. Young Ki Lee thought these might have been templates for embroidery.

Regarding these characters, Harris wrote:

> There are a series of beautifully written words on the reverse. . . . Chinese experts tell me that they show unmistakable Korean brushmanship. Yet they are amazingly excellent examples of Chinese calligraphy. . . . the writing of words is the highest of all Chinese arts. They highly respect the delicate yet virile strokes of the brush, which require so much study that old men are usually the finest exponents of this art of arts. I have a Chinese friend in Taipei . . . who is one of the recognized experts. . . . He has spent 22 years of daily toil, in order to master the involved charms of the Chinese characters.

> We westerners are mere children in the art of writing. Even the finest Spencerian penmanship is of comparative simplicity set over against the rare beauty of Asiatic brushwork. So the words on the Harris map are deeply appreciated by Asiatics, even as we would delight in a complete group of pictures by Michelangelo. With growing knowledge it is inevitable that we Westerners will treasure Chinese words, even as mathematicians prize the beauty of intricate formulas, and artists revere the productions of the masters . . . these words are also hallmarks of the maps' origin and value. . . .

The Koreans also had a language . . . but all official and important works were done using Chinese words. The fact that Chinese words are used throughout the maps is one of those strong proofs that not only were these maps regarded as precious but that they were done under official order.[6]

A new style of calligraphy called "Ch'usa" was introduced to Koreans by Kim Chong-hui (1786-1856),[7] but the calligraphy on this map is not Ch'usa. I have not been able to positively identify the map's calligraphy style. However, it resembles that of the Cao Shu style, which first appeared in China during the Han Dynasty (202 BC-AD 220).[8]

On the world map are large red seals (chops) that surely designate official business, but they are illegible. Red seals like this are not common on this style map, and this is the only one of the *Harris Maps* that has one. McCune displayed a map with five small seals next to the map title and a sixth on the map itself. He stated that they were the seals of previous owners.[9] Harris wrote concerning the seals: "The *Harris Map* book has large red seals and appears to have been accepted as a government approved document."[10]

Yoo pointed out that the left seal represents Yin—the stamp is in white surrounded by red. The right seal represents Yang and is exactly the opposite—red surrounded by white. To make it official, both were needed. There are similar seals, but not exactly the same, on a hand drawn *Ch'onhado* shown in *The History of Cartography*.[11]

In both Korea and China, red has significance and means "full or complete." Red is almost the national color of both Korea and China. Certain localities on the maps are colored. On this world map, Korea and China are elevated into a higher position by putting their names in red round circles. All other countries are designated with squares.

One expert stated that with both Korea and China highlighted, surely the map was done in an era when China and Korea were in harmony. That would place it in the very early Ming Dynasty (1338-1644) as later in that dynasty Korea and China had wars and Korea became the vassal state. The map of Japan in this atlas puts the date as 1471 or later.

The Korean National Library in Seoul has a map similar to the world map in *Harris Map Book 5*. However, while the *Harris Map* is in color, their map is all in brown and has "Korean Colonial Government Library" stamped on it.

As previously stated, a professor with a PhD in Environmental Studies told me that the branch of the tree shown on the right side of *Harris Map 5* is that of a sequoia—the gigantic trees indigenous only to America. He was certain it was a sequoia, saying that he had done research papers on them. That tree is shown on the map as the "Fu Sang Tree." Of course, Fu Sang was what we believe signifies America. This man was surprised to see a sequoia on an old Asian map.

Analysis Done by Young Ki Lee in 2005

Map Book #5

Cover title: *Chidoso Pu Sojang, Pu Yulchang,* (cannot figure the meanings of terms after 'book of maps')

Caption title: *Ch'onha-do*

Printing: Wood Block printing, hand coloring

Probable Date: Before 1767

Atlas size: 31 cm x 19 cm

Map size: 29 cm x 33.5 cm

Material: Mulberry bark paper

Number of Place Names

1. Main Continent: 32, including China and Korea
2. Inner Sea Ring: 56, including Japan and Okinawa
3. Outer Land Ring: 52, with three trees
4. Total: 140

Order of Maps

1. *Ch'onha-do* (*World map*)
2. *Ilbon Kukto* (*Map of Japan*)
3. *Kyongsang-do* (*Map of Kyongsang Province*)
4. *Cholla-do* (*Map of Cholla Province*)
5. *Ch'ungch'ong-do* (*Map of Ch'ungch'ong Province*)
6. *Kangwon-do* (*Map of Kangwon Province*)
7. *Kyonggi* (*Map of Kyonggi Province*)
8. *Hwanghae-do* (*Map of Hwanghae Province*)
9. *P'yongan-do* (*Map of P'yongan Province*)
10. *Hamgyong-do* (*Map of Hamgyong Province*)

Description

1. No similar *Ch'onha-do* has been found in any collection in Korea so far.
2. This atlas does not include a map of Korea, map of China, or map of Okinawa

3. The cover title on the other side, "Sujang pu chido," means "Embroidery base" attached with maps.
4. This set uses both sides of the paper: one side for maps, the other side for Chinese characters for embroidery. Each page has one Chinese character.
5. The seal on the world map is not readable.

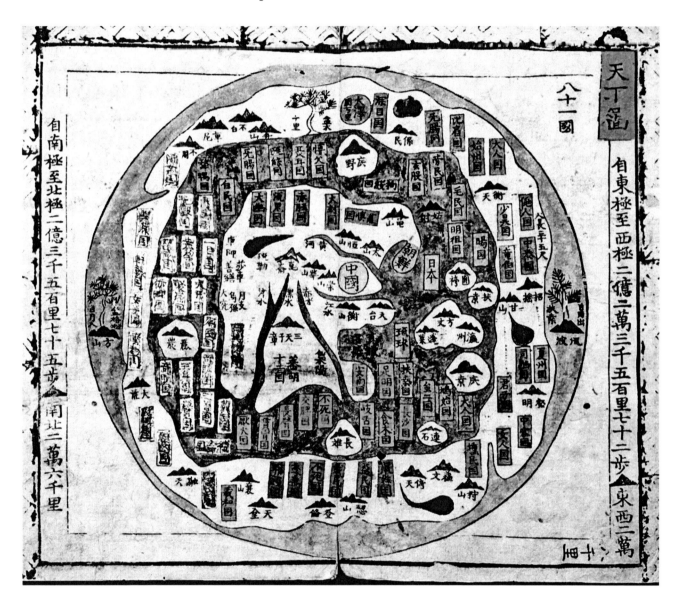

Harris Map Book 6 World Map

Harris Map Book 6 contains thirteen maps: a world map, maps of Korea, Japan, Okinawa, and China, and maps of the eight Korean provinces. This large book has a light brown cover. Some locations are colored in. Perhaps it was a political map. It has special symbols on military installations. It is well preserved.

Dating: Changjin, created in 1787, does not show in this book. Most likely both the wood printing blocks and the map were made **prior to 1787**.

Harris Map Book 6 is unique in that it has two starting places—one on the left side of the atlas and the other on the right. Each cover is followed by a new segment of maps. The four bold characters on one cover read "Dong Hai Cho Sun," the Eastern Sea of Korea.

There are two different styles of writing on the cover. The large characters are hand written. The small, background writing is a genealogy printed with moveable type. Most likely this is just recycling of paper to reinforce the cover. This atlas is unique in that both moveable type print and carved block print are in the same book. (The first recorded printing in Korea by moveable type was AD 1234.)

The printed genealogy is upside down, but lists every member of each generation starting from the 28th generation to the 32nd. With that many generations, Yoo stated that this clan's history spans well over 1,000 years. Few clans in Korea have such long recorded genealogies, indicating that this clan must be a prominent family. The print is difficult to read, but Young Ki Lee believed it to be the Lee family—also known as "Yi," as in the Yi Dynasty.

The world map has no latitude and longitude lines and has distinguishing colors: red in the south, gray in the north, light blue in the east, and white in the west. This *Ch'onhado* states that there were eighty-one countries and also lists information on distances. The right side says, "From East Pole to West Pole it is 200,023,572 steps. From East to West it is 28,000 li." (As stated earlier, a Chinese li is approximately 1/3 mile.) The left side states: "From South Pole to North Pole it is 200,003,575 steps. From South to North, it is 26,000 li."

On the map of China on the right margin, first line, the third (last) entry from the top reads. "Yu controlled water and land, divided into nine provinces." (Yu was the Chinese ruler said to have compiled the *Shan Hai Jing*.)

The map of each province in this atlas also gives a brief history of that region.

Analysis Done by Young Ki Lee in 2005

Map #6

Cover title: *Yodo*

Caption title: *Ch'onha-do*

Printing: Wood Block printing, hand coloring

Probable Date: Late 18th century

Atlas size: 29 cm x 18.5 cm

Map size: 26.5 cm x 31.5 cm

Material: Mulberry bark paper

Number of Place Names

1. Main Continent: 31, including China and Korea
2. Inner Sea Ring: 56, including Japan and Okinawa
3. Outer Land Ring: 52, with three trees
4. Total: 139

Order of Maps

1. *Ch'onha-do* (*World map*)
2. *Chungguk-do* (*Map of China*)
3. *Tongguk P'alto Taech'ong-do* (*Map of Korea*)
4. *Ilbon* (*Map of Japan*)
5. *Ryuguk-kuk* (*Map of Okinawa*)
6. *Kyonggi-do* (*Map of Kyonggi Province*)
7. *Kangwon-do* (*Map of Kangwon Province*)
8. *Ch'ungch'ong-do* (*Map of Ch'ungch'ong Province*)
9. *Kyongsang-do* (*Map of Kyongsang Province*)
10. *Cholla-do* (*Map of Cholla Province*)
11. *Hwanghae-do* (*Map of Hwanghae Province*)
12. *P'yongan-do* (*Map of P'yongan Province*)
13. *Hamgyong-do* (*Map of Hamgyong Province*)

Description

1. Uses same wood block as *Harris Map Book 2*. See p. 166 of Lee, Chan. *Han'guk ui Ko chido*, 1st ed., Seoul, Pomusa, 1991.

2. There is a second cover title: *Tonghae Choson*.

3. As in *Harris Map Book 2*, this *Ch'onha-do* only has information about the distance between East and West, North and South.

4. P'alsibil-kuk, which means "eighty-one countries," appears on the left side of the caption title.

5. Each provincial map has a brief history of the province. (This information could be a good clue to judge the probable date.)

6. The world map has four colors: red in south portion, gray in north, light blue in east, and white in west.

7. Right side of the *Ch'onha-do* states: "From East Pole to West Pole it is 200,023, 572 steps. From East to West it is 28,000 li.

8. Left side of *Ch'onha-do* states: "From South Pole to North Pole it is 200,003,575 steps. From South to North, it is 26,000 li."

9. The back of this atlas was made of scratch paper once used for the Lee family genealogical table, but which branch of the Lee family and what generations are unknown.

Cover of *Harris Map Book 6* shows a genealogy.

Harris Map Book 7 World Map

Harris Map Book 7 contains ten maps: a world map, a map of China, and maps of the eight Korean provinces. Korea, Japan, and Okinawa are not included.

Dating: The wood blocks appear to have been made **pre-1767**.

This book is unique in that each province lists the number of jurisdictions (kwan) in that province. The provincial maps in *Harris Map Book 1* also show numbers of jurisdictions, but several of those numbers are different from those on this map. This would imply that the wood blocks for the two books were carved at different times. We have not yet followed up on this.

This is another large atlas with a dark cover. There is no color on the maps. The world map has no latitude and longitude lines. All eight Korean provinces are depicted.

Analysis Done by Young Ki Lee in 2005

Map Book #7

Cover title: No cover title

Caption title: *Ch'onha-do*

Printing: Wood Block printing, no color

Probable Date: Early 18th century Atlas size: 32.5 cm x 18 cm

Map size: 28.5 cm x 34.5 cm

Material: Mulberry bark paper

Number of Place Names:

1. Main Continent: 32, including China and Korea
2. Inner Sea Ring: 56, including Japan and Okinawa
3. Outer Land Ring: 52, with three trees
4. Total: 140

Order of Maps

1. *Ch'onha-do (World Map)*
2. *Chungguk-do (Map of China)*
3. *Cholla-do (Map of Cholla Province)*
4. *Ch'ungch'ong-do (Map of Ch'ungch'ong Province)*
5. *Kyonggi (Map of Kyonggi Province)*
6. *Hwanghae-do (Map of Hwanghae Province)*
7. *P'yongan-do (Map of P'yongan Province)*
8. *Hamgyong-do (Map of Hamgyong Province)*
9. *Kangwon-do (Map of Kangwon Province)*
10. *Kyongsang-do (Map of Kyongsang Province)*

Description

1. No map of Korea is in this set.
2. Eastern portion of *Map of Kyongsang Province* is missing.
3. Each provincial map has the number of jurisdictions in handwriting. This information could be used to assess the probable date. (Compare these numbers with those in *Harris Map Book 1*. They are not identical.)

Kyonggi Province: 37 kwan
Ch'ungch'ong Province: 54 kwan
Cholla Province: 57 kwan
Kyongsang Province: 69 kwan
Hwanghae Province: 23 kwan
P'yongan Province: 42 kwan
Kangwon Province: 26 kwan
Hamgyong Province: 22 kwan

Appendix

Is the Library of Congress Hiding Information about Chinese Preceding Columbus to the Americas?—January 2010
by Charlotte Harris Rees

I am certainly in favor of the Library of Congress publicly displaying old Asian maps. For too long their collection has been kept in the vault. On January 12, 2010, they started displaying a 1602 map in Chinese *http://www.loc.gov/index. html*. What angers me is that the Library of Congress is touting this as "The First Map in Chinese Showing the Americas"—especially when they know better. I believe that this is part of their effort to hide from the public that there are pre-Columbian Asian maps of the Americas.

In 2003 and once since then I, as part of a small group, was shown a map in the vault of the map division of the Library of Congress. That map has both Asian and European style writing on it and shows Asia and parts of North America including Alaska. The map division told us then that the map was carbon dated to the late 14th century. Despite the fact that they have owned that map at least fifty years, the Library of Congress has ignored repeated requests from various sources for them to either fully verify it or deny its veracity.

Furthermore, my family owns the *Dr. Hendon Harris, Jr. Map Collection*. The world maps in our collection are known as *Ch'onhado* in Korean or *Tian Xia Tu* in Chinese. In Chinese this means "(Everything) Under Heaven Map," which is understood by Chinese to mean "the whole earth."

Even in Korean map books, this style of map was produced in Chinese script. The maps show both North and South America. For the past seven years I have researched about this map. My books are endorsed by prestigious scholars and I lecture internationally on this topic.

In late 2007 the Library of Congress co-authored *Cartographia: Mapping Civilizations*. In that book it recognized the *Ch'onhado* as a genuine world map—but dated it 1592. That text does not explain how they arrived at that date—which ironically is exactly 100 years after Columbus. It is remarkable that they should be able to arrive at such a precise date, especially since *The History of Cartography* (which the kind people at the Library of Congress told me was the "Bible" on maps) calls this a "seemingly primitive map" and states that this map "made a silent and utterly unnoted debut at a date we cannot pin down even to the century." That book quotes early modern commentator Yi Ik Seup, who stated it was "from time immemorial."

I had spoken at the Library of Congress in 2005 and was invited to speak there again in 2008 after the release of my book *Secret Maps of the Ancient World*. That speech was advertised on the Internet and in Washington, D.C. newspapers—but was suddenly cancelled without explanation. My inside sources tell me that the cancellation came from "high up." (Incidentally, I have since lectured at University of London; Stanford University; University. of Maryland; Simon Fraser University, Vancouver, B. C.; and other universities—all with good reviews.)

I sent a pleasant e-mail to the Chief of the Geography and Maps Division, who had previously answered all my e-mails and to whom I had given personal copies of my books, asking why in choosing a date for the *Ch'onhado* in *Cartographia* they had ignored the reputable text *Old Maps of Korea* by Korean Library Science Research Institute (which is found in his division). That book states that the *Ch'onhado* was old in 1402 when they introduced the *Kangnido*. (As stated previously, that map is in Chinese.) In addition, in 1947 *Imago Mundi* Japanese scholar, Dr. Hiroshi Nakamura, contended that the *Ch'onhado* was Chinese in origin and was in existence at least by the seventh century. Furthermore, Dr. Joseph Needham of Cambridge quoted a Chinese text from the third century that mentioned an incident involving that style map in the 18th century BC. Since then my e-mails to this chief are unanswered.

I have waited years for them to verify the 14th century map in their vault. I brushed off the cancellation of my speech by thinking that they must have had a good reason. I also rationalized that since *Cartographia: Mapping Civilizations* is about many different maps, the Library of Congress might have inadvertently missed information in that text about one. However, now that I have laid the proofs on their lap and yet they are still presenting this Ricci map as the "First Map in Chinese Showing the Americas," I cannot help but conclude that The Library of Congress is **purposely** hiding evidence that Asians beat Columbus to America.

I would rather live in peace than start a fight—especially with the Library of Congress, one of the most influential organizations in the world. However, if I do not bring this to light, who will? Sometimes in the lives of all of us we must choose truth over peace.

Ancient Chinese Wrote About America's Big Trees

When my father died, among the books in his library I found a copy of *National Geographic* from January 1917. The lead article in that issue is titled "Our Big Trees Saved." It is about the sequoia trees in California , which are native to America.

The article tells that in 1916 the US Congress appropriated $50,000 for the purchase of land in order to save those trees which were being harvested for their valued wood. Congress learned that the owners, though sympathetic to the government purchase and preservation of the trees:

> could not fairly part with their sequoia trees except on condition that adjacent property be purchased also, the supplementary lands bringing the price up to $70,000. [Even that was a generous concession since the timber on the land was valued at $156,000.]

At that time the US government received a six month option to complete the purchase of the property for $70,000. However, late that year:

> With the expiration of the option only three weeks off, and with no prospect of being able to secure the necessary additional appropriation of $20,000 from Congress during its pre-holiday session, the Department of the Interior had practically lost all hope of saving these most highly prized of all trees for the American people.

> In this predicament one of the officials of the department recalled the splendid work which has been done for a number of years by the National Geographic Society in stimulating public interest in the preservation of the nation's playgrounds…

In short order the half a million members of National Geographic Society provided the needed $20,000. Within days:

> The purchase was completed and the title of the Big Trees passed to the U.S. Government on January 17, 1917.

The rest of that 1917 article goes on to tell of the glories of those trees.

> In the scenic heart of the Sequoia National Park, the only section of the magnificent 160,000 acre playground situated in California which is at the present time accessible to motor driven and horse-drawn vehicles, stands a group of trees, the Sequoia Washingtoniana, known as the Giant Forest, and

in this forest grow the loftiest and most venerable living things that Nature has produced.

> The Sequoia National Park was constituted a government preserve to safeguard these very trees, some of which were 2000 years old when the Christian era dawned.

In another section of that article it was stated:

> As a hunter keeps a record of the bears he has killed by the notches in his gunstock, so the big tree keeps an account of the years it has lived by rings concealed within its trunk....John Muir [famous naturalist] counted four thousand rings from the heart out of one fallen giant.

The article relates:

> Who could replace them? Not man, for never yet in all his existence has he had continuity of purpose enough to plan 2,000 years ahead. The mutations of time in twenty centuries leave only here and there a silent monument to speak of the past...

> Yet when unnumbered thousands of Egyptian slaves were laboriously transporting the stones for Cheops across the Nile Valley these hoary old veterans of the California mountains were sturdy saplings.

> The human progress they must have witnessed! In their early youth the children of Israel were wandering through the Wilderness of Sin. When the Star of Bethlehem shone down over that lowly manger in Judea, proclaiming the second deliverance of mankind, who knows but that these monarchs of the California forest which have just been rescued from the woodman's axe joined in singing "Glory to the Highest," and the winds of the East swept over the West!

That beautiful and emotionally written article inspired me and my family to visit the Seguoia National Forest a couple of years ago. It was an awe inspiring visit. However, in addition to the *National Geographic* article, I also had other interests in seeing those majestic trees.

For years it has been debated what the Fu Sang tree in ancient Chinese literature really was. In 2009 after I had spoken at a university in Rhode Island, a PhD with specialty in environmental studies came up to ask me about the sequoia tree on my father's map. I was shocked by his statement that it was a sequoia. At that time I realized that the map showed a tree on the right side. Next to the tree is the caption: "Fu Sang Tree. The sun and moon rise here."

Dave and Charlotte Rees at the Sequoia National Forest

I realized that the depiction seemed to be of some type of conifer and that there was a specific layout of the needles, but other than that did not give it much thought. However, that day the PhD told me that he had studied in depth and written papers on the sequoia and he was sure what was tree on the map was a sequoia.

Several different Chinese writings describe the enormous trees in the country of Fu Sang, which we believe to be America. Edward Payson Vining in his 1885 text *An Inglorious Columbus* quoted Chinese author Tong Fan Tso who lived 200 BC.

> At the east of the Eastern Sea, the shores of the country of Fu–sang is found. If, after landing on these shores, the journey is continued by land toward the east for a distance of then thousand li, a sea of blue color is reached, vast, immense and boundless. The countryof Fu–sang extends ten thousand li upon each of its sides....

> Great forests are found filled with trees...similar to that of those which is call chin (certain coniferous trees). They attain a height of several times ten thousand

cubits, and it takes two thousand people to reach their arms around one of them. These trees grow two and two from common roots and mutually sustain each other… their leaves and their fruit are similar to those of mulberry of China. The fruit, of exquisite flavor and of reddish colour, appears but very rarely…but once in nine thousand years.

Vining comments:

> The exaggeration of the proportion of the fu-sang tree is evidently nothing but hyperbole: but it may be remarked that this tree is described as resembling the mulberry in its leaves, and chin tree in its form: this last being a species of conifer of which the wood is used in the manufacture of arrows. This description, although not having great botanical precision, reminds one of the Wellingtonia of California, which may be the last remains of an immense forest.

> The indication of a breadth of ten thousand li for the country of Fu–sang shows that it was a true continent; and if we do not believe that this curious account of another ocean, found to the east, beyond the vast territory, should be applied to the Atlantic, it still may be thought that America was better known to the Chinese before the Christian era.

My father and I both discussed in our books many other arguments that the legendary Chinese "Fu Sang" was America. The width of Fu Sang given thousands of years ago by this Chinese writer is almost the exact width of North America. However, he also mentions that Fu Sang is that wide on all sides – surely this could reference North America. If the Chinese writer was referring to North America, he is correct that to the east of the continent is another immense ocean – the Atlantic.

Vining is correct in that there is surely hyperbole in the statement regarding the size of the trees. Numerous Chinese writers mentioned the enormous trees found in Fu Sang. If the Chinese did indeed make it to North America at early dates, they likely saw those enormous trees. Trees of this size are found nowhere else on earth. This description of the Fu Sang tree tied with the drawing of it on the oldest maps of this style still in existence certainly points to sequoia.

Some writers have tried to make the Fu Sang tree red Indian corn because of the references to the red fruit. However, note that Tong Fan Tso said that the fruit came only every 9000 years. Therefore, he probably never saw the fruit and quite likely this was another hyperbole indicating that it did not bear fruit. When I asked about fruit at the park, I was told there was none.

It does puzzle me how the leaves could look like mulberry leaves and yet the tree be a conifer –especially when the drawing of the Fu Sang tree on our map shows needles.

Dave, Daniel and Charlotte Rees at the Sequoia National Forest

I checked on whether sequoia grew multiple trees from one root as Tong Fan Tso alleged for the large trees. I learned that a feature of Coast Redwoods is that they often have multiple shoots (suckers) growing from their basal roots. Among conifers this feature is almost unique to redwoods. Tree botanist Philip Mulholland of the UK stated recently in an e-mail to me. "I think it is very exciting that Tong Fan Tso was able to describe this rare and distinctive feature of a conifer tree native to the Pacific Coast of North America."

Whether or not you choose to believe that the American sequoia was the Chinese Fu Sang tree, it should still be on your bucket list to visit that park.

The 1917 *National Geographic* article stated:

> Dead indeed must be the soul of the man whose heart is not quickened, whose spirit is not moved to reverence, whose thoughts do not reach out and beyond, and whose inmost being does not look up through nature to nature's God, amid such surroundings as these!

As I stood there and viewed those magnificent trees, I agreed.

BY CHARLOTTE REES

Secret Maps of the Ancient World

Did the Chinese beat Columbus to the New World?

October in central Virginia is marked with pumpkins, Columbus Day and Harvest Festivals. Columbus Day has not always been a part of Americana, however. It was not until the 20th century that it became a national holiday. It was introduced to most people with little fanfare. Why would federal employees complain? For them it is a break from work. For everyone else, it made little difference.

Many people over the years, though, have asked "Why should Columbus be honored for discovering America when everyone acknowledges that there were already millions of people here when he arrived?"

Most texts of American history start with the arrival of Columbus. But almost everyone agrees that people have lived in the Americas for at least 4000 years. So what happened to the rest of that history?

That question led me on a journey of discovery in which I have come to believe that my father's thesis of Chinese people inhabiting the American continent thousands of years before the Nina, Pinta and Santa Maria came ashore was too obvious to be ignored.

The story begins with an ancient map in a shop in Korea . . .

The map on the left, now known as the "Harris Map," was found by Rees' father in 1972. The red dots in the center mark China and Korea. It indicates that the sun rises on the right side of the map and sets on the left. Fu Sang is shown on the far right.

The map on the right is an illustration by David A. Deal that helps give perspective to the Harris Map. Find Africa on the left of the middle section then move east first to China and then to the Americas. Distances in oceans are not to scale.

A quest begins

In 1972, the year that my husband Dave and I moved to Central Virginia from Chicago, my father, Dr. Hendon Harris, Jr., found an unusual ancient map in an antique shop in Korea. For thousands of years, Chinese literature discussed Fu Sang, a beautiful land east of them. There on the old map in my father's hands, Fu Sang was on the location where today we see the Americas.

My father, a third-generation Baptist missionary, was born in interior China and as early as he spoke English, he also learned Chinese. He was familiar with Chinese classical writings and on seeing the map realized that it showed a location of the supposedly mythical Fu Sang.

A year later, my father wrote a book of almost 800 pages on that topic titled *The Asiatic Fathers of America: Chinese Discovery and Colonization of Ancient America*. However, in the 70s, few accepted his theories that Chinese had traveled by sea to the Americas starting around 2200 B.C. and were the ancestors of the American Indians.

My father died suddenly of a stroke in 1981. My six siblings and I divided his belongings but decided to keep his map collection together and some day have it authenticated. By then the collection had grown to seven similar map books, and Father had located a few others in prestigious museums around the world. At that time, all those maps were considered imaginary, though they were normally found in serious government books in which every other map was real.

Soon after father's death, I and my siblings were preoccupied with our careers and our own young families. Soon the maps were forgotten under my brother's bed. Occasionally at family reunions, someone would mention them, but we had neither the time nor inclination to take to be authenticated.

The quest begins anew

However, in January 2003, only days after my husband and I retired and 22 years after Father died, I read a book written by Gavin Menzies, which contends that the Chinese had reached America about 70 years before Columbus.

By that point of my life, I was about the same age that my father had been when he wrote his book. Having lived through several decades, history had new significance to me. Reading Menzies' book caused me to wonder whether my father could have

been right. At my prompting, my brother flew from California with the maps. Together we took them to the Library of Congress where they stayed for three years while experts studied them.

The more I researched, the more information came to light. *The Asiatic Fathers of America* was published in Taiwan, and only a few copies had been distributed, so I was amazed to find it mentioned by several recent authors. Copies of his book that one sister had sold to a book dealer for $1 each in 1981 were selling in 2003 on the Internet for $40 each. (Currently, they sell for up to $200 each.)

Rees spoke about her findings to the Library of Congress in 2005 at the Zheng He Symposium.

I was also astonished to discover that someone who read *The Asiatic Fathers of America* went on an extensive search to find my father, then wrote a book in 1978 about Father and his theory. That man never found Father, but added information about him in 1985 and 1989 revisions. In that book, one chapter about ancient Chinese literature was written by a Dr. Cyclone Covey.

In 2003, through the Internet and then a phone call, I was able to locate Dr. Covey, history professor emeritus at Wake Forest University. My first question was whether he knew of my father, Hendon Harris. (Unknown to me, Covey had quoted Father in four of his own books!) Thinking that one more question would end my search on this issue, I asked Covey if recent research had proved my father wrong. Covey's reply was that, to the contrary, there was now much more evidence that Harris was right. Covey offered to mentor me in my search and suggested a few books for me to read.

Covey affirmed that my father was the first in recent times to associate this map with the Americas. Over the past five years, I have consulted him frequently. In 2005, I gave a speech at the Library of Congress about my father's research. Then, realizing that few people would want to read any 800-page text, in 2006 I came out with an abridged version of *The Asiatic Fathers of America*.

The birth of a book

As an investigative reporter would, since early 2003 I have been gathering together the research of many highly qualified academics on this topic. My quest was to prove to myself whether my father was right. The amount of evidence is astounding. (I have now read more than 200 books and articles on this subject.)

My search has led me through studies in science, archeology, oceanography, philosophy, anthropology, art, linguistics and mathematics. Each researcher thought that his area of expertise was conclusive proof. However, by bringing together the findings in

THE EVIDENCE THE CHINESE WERE HERE FIRST

My research was in two main areas. First, were the Chinese even capable in 2200 to 2000 B.C. of crossing the Pacific, and is there tangible evidence that they did so? Secondly, do the prototypes of these maps really date that far back? In *Secret Maps*, I present my findings but let the reader decide.

Here's the evidence. What do you think?

Two hundred Indian tribes have been tested and all show founding DNA from Asia. Confucius in 500 B.C. wrote of wild tribes to the east of China and of people crossing oceans. One "ah ha" moment for me was studying archeology of China and seeing pictures of their reconstructed ancient villages. The houses were teepees or round houses, which are very similar to those of American Indians. An ancient Chinese skull had been reconstructed as is currently done on CSI. The head looked just like an American Indian. However, the Chinese author of that book made no mention of possible connection to our Indians.

Another Chinese archeology book mentions (with no explanation) that peanuts dating to before 2000 B.C., but native to the Americas, have been found in more than one Chinese archeological excavation. Ancient Chinese writing has been found in multiple places in the Americas—even some dating to pre-1800 B.C. in Colorado. My research led to hundreds of items either in Asia or the Americas that appear to have been found on the wrong continent.

But back to the ancient Chinese classics that described Fu Sang. Writings from 2000 B.C. seemed aware of the Grand Canyon and animals native to America. Around 300 B.C., a writer in China stated that Fu Sang had huge trees (the redwoods?), was 10,000 li (3300 miles) wide, then one comes to another big blue ocean. That is almost the exact width of North America. How could they know that without having come?

Warm ocean currents in the Pacific push logs or boats east to the Americas and then down the coast. There is a return current at the equator. An Asian parasite found in a dig in Mexico had to have come by sea because it could not have survived the cold northern trek.

Last year a researcher from London came to Forest to visit me and take pictures of a few native Chinese plants that grow wild in this area of Virginia, including ginseng and rhododendron and paulownia and mimosa trees. No one seems to know how they got here. There are still many mysteries, and we certainly do not have all the answers.

many different disciplines, there is finally so much evidence that it can no longer be ignored. Sometimes I refer to it as a "tsunami of evidence" as even more information continues to come in.

My book, *Secret Maps of the Ancient World*, just out in June, is garnering attention around the world. Since 2005, I have been on television and featured in newspapers, magazines (even in Beijing) and on National Public Radio. During an interview by NPR, the commentator from California told me she was trying to envision how I did my research. She asked if I was reading books and taking notes as I sat on my bed. It sounded like she imagined someone from Forest, Virginia, sitting in a log cabin in the woods!

I had to laugh as I told her that I have an office in my home with a phone, computer, bookcases, files, and file cabinets. My husband and I made over a dozen trips to the Library of Congress in Washington, D.C. I have bought many books (some in other languages) on the Internet and also secured numerous others through my local library by inter-library loan. With today's resources, even a small person in a small place can do intense research on an obscure subject.

I now communicate with several of the authors whose books I have studied. Europeans and Australians as well as Asians and Native Americans are very interested in our history. I am astounded that in the past 12 months my Web site, www.HarrisMaps.com, has received more than 107,000 hits that come in around the clock. My contacts circle the globe.

In *Secret Maps of the Ancient World*, I try to bring history and my search alive. One reviewer compared this book to a *National Treasure* movie script. The overriding statement people have after reading the book is amazement at the amount of documented research and the comment, "This makes sense!"

My interest in Columbus is not to discredit what he accomplished by crossing the Atlantic but rather to introduce new insights. Some ask, "What does it matter?" It matters because in our land of freedom of information, we need to know the truth of our history. SM

For more information about Rees and her book, go to www.HarrisMaps.com. *Secret Maps of the Ancient World* is in stock in Lynchburg at Givens Books, Heritage Books and New Life Books. It can be ordered through most local bookstores worldwide and is available on many sites on the Internet.

A book signing will be held Oct. 25, 1-3 p.m. at Givens Books, 2236 Lakeside Dr. in Lynchburg.

Rees hugs Chinese students in 2006 at a Summer English Camp in Xi'an, China.

life

CHINA DAILY 中国日报 CHINADAILY.COM.CN/LIFE

FRIDAY, JULY 9, 2010 | PAGE 18

Tomorrow

Lost in translation

Lijiang has some of the most impressive Chinglish signs in the country, both amusing and educating.

Maps, money and DNA

Q: Why are the ideas in your book so controversial?

A: It's not easy to rewrite history. I'm not a PhD, and if I were to pursue a PhD, I'd need university and academic mentors who supported the research. Most experts on the discovery of America have invested their lives and careers documenting a different view, a Eurocentric view.

It wasn't always that way, though. I have seen copies of US history textbooks from around 1905, which say that the Chinese have been in America for at least 1,000 years. So this isn't a new idea. But by around 1910 there were new academic pressures, and then came the Columbus Day national holiday. After that, school kids in the US stopped hearing about Chinese coming to America.

Q: It seems that a lot of Chinese scholars are as reluctant to embrace the idea as US scholars are. Why?

A: There is immense interest here. But it can't be proved, especially with Chinese documents, because, soon after the voyages of Zheng He, there was a tremendous reaction against these outside adventures and the strain such shipbuilding put on the country's economy. Ships, maps, records were all destroyed and China became an inward-looking society for centuries. That's why it's easier to find ancient maps that tell the story in Korea, where they were not destroyed by government order, than it is in China.

Q: The US Library of Congress recently exhibited a famous map made by Matteo Ricci, the Italian Jesuit, which the Library said was the first known map of the Americas with Chinese inscriptions. You challenged that publicly.

A: It was a surprising thing for the Library of Congress to say. Many people doing research in this area have seen older maps of the Americas with Chinese writing. One of them is in the Library of Congress' own collection, though

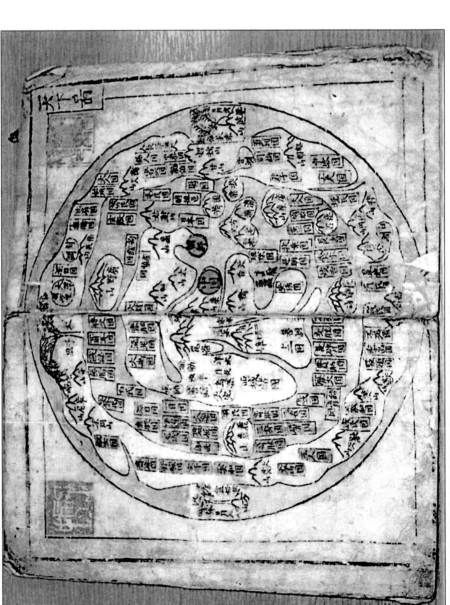

World Map in *Book 5 — Dr Hendon M Harris, Jr Collection, from The Asiatic Fathers of America.*

Nailing their

colors to the mast

The treasure trove of seafaring knowledge amassed by the Chinese over the centuries is at the heart of a debate over the extent of their ancient voyages, **Mike Peters** reports

A bright-eyed, middle-aged woman from the state of Virginia, United States, sits waiting for her next interview in a Lido-area hotel lobby. She's a retired social worker, a no-nonsense lady who speaks quietly and deliberately. But she is in town to help answer the question: Did medieval Chinese navigators reach the Americas years before Christopher Columbus? Just a few years ago, Charlotte Harris Rees started thinking that her late father might have held the key to one of history's great mysteries.

Few people expect ever to own documents that could change world history," Harris writes in her 2008 book, *Secret Maps of the Ancient World*, "and neither did we. Yet for decades, under my brother's bed, lay ancient Asian maps that we, our father's seven children, inherited from him. Some believe that they may contain a secret of the ancient world".

That possibility brought Rees to Asia this month for two weeks of conferences and speeches. Her first stop focused on Zheng He (1371–1435), the 15th-century Chinese admiral who was dispatched by Emperor Zhu Di to "proceed all the way to the end of the Earth".

An international conference this week in Malaka, Malaysia — a seafarer's crossroads for centuries that was an important base for Zheng He — explored questions about Africa. Zheng certainly got there, but exactly where and the extent of his fleet's settlements and activities have engaged curious scholars for centuries.

The question that excites Rees, however, is whether Zheng He — and perhaps his Chinese predecessors — sailed to America as well.

Academics have batted around that idea for centuries, but it wasn't until Gavin Menzies published his bestselling book, *1421: The Year China Discovered the World*, eight years ago that the debate became an international firestorm. One of the sparks landed on Rees, who read *1421* with amazement and realized that the author was trying to connect the same dots her father had followed in his research.

"When I was a social worker straight out of college, many of my clients in Oklahoma were American Indians who looked very Asian to me," she says today. "But the idea of Chinese coming to America 4,200 years ago in boats sounded pretty far-fetched then".

But her father, Hendon M Harris Jr, a child of Christian missionaries who worked in several regions of China, was fascinated by the possibility. He picked up references to ancient Chinese navigators from several sources, including the ancient classic *Shan Hai Jing* (Collection of the Mountains and Seas), said to have been written in 2,200 BC and quoted in Chinese history and literature ever since.

The *Shan Hai Jing* tells of Chinese travel to the four corners of the earth, says Rees, "including a beautiful land to the east of China named Fu Sang."

Then one day in 1972, Harris was browsing in an antique shop in Shouth Korea, looking for gifts for his family in the United States. He was examining the wares on display when the shopkeeper said, "I have a map in the back. Would you like to see that?"

"Father wasn't really into collecting maps — not then! — but he said, 'Yes,' the daughter says. And when the map was spread out, as he recounted to his children years later, "he had to sit down because he felt himself shaking all over".

What Harris saw was a world map block-printed in an ancient Shang (16th century to 11th century BC) Chinese style, with China at the center and a circular continent looping around the edges of the page. He immediately related this to the Fu Sang of the *Shan Hai Jing*. In subsequent years Harris found copies of similar maps in the collections of museums and universities.

However, opinion is divided over the identity of Fu Sang, many believe it refers to somewhere in America;

Dr Hendon M Harris, Jr.

IF YOU GO

Charlotte Harris Rees will speak about her research at two public forums in Beijing:

• Today, July 9, 9-11 am, National Library of China

• Monday, July 19, Tsinghua University. 9-11 am; Rees will repeat the presentation she made at the International Zheng He conference in Malaysia. Two other presenters from that conference will also speak.

under him with the discovery of the world beyond China, Harris argues that Zheng He set sail with maps made from information acquired hundreds, even thousands of years earlier.

Charlotte Harris Rees finds that argument persuasive. Her speech in Malaka this week was titled *Zheng He's Inheritance*, and she told her audience that "starting a study of Chinese sea travel with Zheng He is like beginning a study of space travel with a trip to Mars".

Chinese seafaring was refined over centuries, she believes. "Zheng He could not have been as successful as he was, without the treasure trove of knowledge and invention amassed by the Chinese over many years of sea travel."

An illustration from the July 2005 issue of National Geographic compares Zheng He's largest ships to European vessels of the same era. The article contends that the Chinese admiral's fleet contained up to 62 *baochuan*, or treasure ships, that measured 122 m by 52 m.

"You could fit all of Columbus' ships and all of Vasco da Gama's on a single deck of a ship that size," Rees says in awe. Rees talks about her father's research today with the passion of a religious convert. She talks of ancient Chinese shipwrecks off the US Pacific coast. Of maps Columbus and Magellan are said to have used on their voyages. Of DNA testing on Native Americans, with undisputed links to ancient Chinese.

So is she convinced that Chinese adventurers, not Columbus, "discovered America"?

"I don't pretend to know the answers," she says, smiling. "But as we find more and more evidence, I think we have to keep trying to put it together until we do know."

while others claim it is more likely to be Japan.

A year later, Harris wrote *The Asiatic Fathers of America: Chinese Discovery and Colonization of Ancient America*. It got some notice in academic circles, but it was never the pop-culture phenomenon of *1421*, though its premise was much more controversial.

For while Menzies' book credits the voyages of Zheng He and the admirals

A: Well, it's true that many Western scholars are invested in the history of the European discovery of America. But it may be a matter of money, too. In May 2003, the Library of Congress completed their purchase of the Waldseemuller Map of the world for $10 million. Five million came from Congress and the other $5 million from donors. According to their 2003 press release that map was the "first image of the outline of the continents of the world as we know them today — Martin Waldseemuller's monumental 1507 map". That indeed is a beautiful map. However, if the Library of Congress now, only seven years later, admits that any other map that shows the American continents predates the Waldseemuller, then perhaps Congress and the donors who helped purchase the Waldseemuller will complain their money was misspent.

Many scholars contend that since the Waldseemuller and other European maps showed the Pacific Coast of the Americas before Europeans had been there, that they had to be copied from earlier maps.

Q: People who read your book, your father's book and Gavin Menzies' book can easily be overwhelmed by all of the evidence you cite. But critics contend most of it is circumstantial. Of everything you've seen and learned about, what has been the most convincing evidence for you?

A: DNA evidence, which is quite recent. We've known for a long time that the "Chinese blue spot", which appears on the buttocks of babies and then disappears, is also seen at birth in many Native American communities. Now we know that five distinct genetic markers match ancient Chinese with modern Native Americans. That's evidence that you can take to court and win.

Charlotte Harris Rees in Beijing.

The Truth Endures

Charlotte Harriss Rees

Published in *US-China Review*, Summer 2011

My father, Dr. Hendon M. Harris, Jr., and I are but two in a series of people who have argued that Chinese arrived to the Americas by sea before Columbus. In fact, thousands of books and articles have been written on different aspects of this subject, and it's been debated since the 1700s.

In some of these texts the contribution is just a few sentences, such as in *Molecular Photofitting,* in which Dr. Tony Frudakis contends that unexplainably there is DNA considered Native American in Central Asia—in large enough quantity to show up in a pie graph. Since Native American DNA is derived from Asia—yet different—Dr. Frudakis thought that perhaps this implied a reverse migration after a period of years in the new world. Considering the ocean currents and Chinese writing about going back and forth, this is entirely possible.

Or perhaps the few sentences would be from *Behind the Scenes in Hopi Land* by M. W. Billingsley who wrote: "the interpreter would reveal the history of the Hopi people which began in a far away country across the great waters, where their villages and country was surrounded

Raymond and Darius Williams in this photo are Tlingit American Indians from Alaska.

with great walls on the tops of which great cows drawing wagons passed back and forth. The interpreter continued the descriptions of their migrations down to the present locations." As I read that, my mind went back to the city walls of Xi'an, on top of which my friends and I rode bikes in the summer of 2006. The ancient city walls in China are as wide as many streets. Perhaps each author's contribution alone is small, but together they form a tsunami of evidence.

I have been told that my father was the first in recent years to realize the significance of the round style of world map (pictured on the cover). In 1973, in an era when major U.S. universities scoffed at those who believed something other than that Native Americans originated and developed on this continent with no outside intervention, my father, Dr. Hendon M. Harris, Jr. wrote *The Asiatic Fathers of America,* citing his maps and much other academic evidence suggesting that Chinese arrived by sea to the Americas starting around 2000 BC.

Another unique contribution was that his book brought to light the many Chinese literary references to Fu Sang that show up on the map on the American coastline. Several early Chinese writers mentioned the huge trees (giant redwoods?) they found in Fu Sang. One from the third century BC stated that Fu Sang was 10,000 li (3,300 miles) wide (almost the exact width of North America), then one came to another expansive blue ocean.

For many years I was a skeptic about my father's book. In early 2003, I read Gavin Menzies' book *1421: The Year China Discovered America.* That book caused me to question whether my father could have been right. I sent Gavin an email congratulating him on his book and telling him about my family's maps and my father's research.

Meanwhile, my brother and I took our maps to the Library of Congress where they stayed for three years while they were studied. Though the map division treated me kindly, no one noticed my comings and goings until late 2004 when Gavin (whom they recognized as a *NY Times* best-selling author) came to see the maps. I had to limit the number of people who could be there while Gavin was viewing them, then had to briefly explain what Gavin had come to see and what I thought it meant.

On that occasion I had a brief private audience with Gavin in which he warned me of the many difficulties ahead and encouraged me to think big. He told me then that he thought there was not one chance in 100 million that my father was wrong. That was also when I got to know Dr. Hwa-Wei Lee, Chief of the Asian Division of the Library, who has since endorsed my books and opened many doors for me.

When Gavin was asked to speak at the Library of Congress in May 2005, he agreed to do so if they would let me and a handful of others also speak. A Caucasian professor from Singapore tried to have Gavin and all of us even loosely associated with him expelled from that symposium. Dr. Hwa-Wei Lee replied, "This is America. We have freedom of speech here. We will let them speak."

The Library brought in extra security for that event. Because Gavin has a higher profile than I do, he has gone through a lot more opposition than I have and has experienced malicious attacks around the world. When I was scheduled to speak at Stanford University, the man and his group who attempted to cause problems at the Library of Congress wrote two letters to the president of Stanford doing his best to stop me. Stanford let me speak.

I also consider Dr. S. L. Lee, Dr. Kent Deng, Chao Chien, and Dr. John Ruskamp, who contributed articles to this issue, as friends. In July 2010 the first three men and I all spoke at the Zheng He Symposium in Melaka, Malaysia, then later at Tsinghua University in Beijing, China's Harvard. At one point, my luggage was lost and S.L.'s wife Theresa loaned me the silk jacket off her back so I did not have to lecture in the T-shirt I'd been traveling in. Both Kent and Chao allowed me to quote them in my book. In 2008, Chao proofread the Chinese in my manuscript. In 2009 Kent booked a lecture for me at the University of London. While we are all independent warriors, we are inspired to assist each other as we are able.

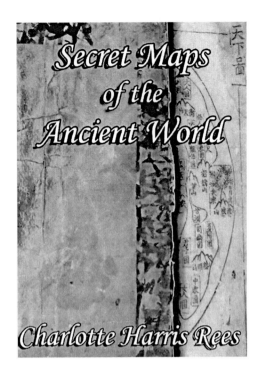

Though at first skeptical about my father's research, my first contribution to this study was to honestly examine his book, *The Asiatic Fathers of America,* and then to bring it out in an abridged (800 pages down to 150) version in 2006. My second contribution was in 2008—my own book, *Secret Maps of the Ancient World,* which springboards from my father's and includes much new evidence. No book other than *Secret Maps of the Ancient World* explores this subject back to the dawn of Chinese history, 2000 BC, while bringing hundreds of academic sources together and explaining them in layman's language. For those who want to study this subject further, read *Secret Maps of the Ancient World* as an overview, then read through the books and articles in its bibliography.

The senior statesman on the topic of the early arrival of Chinese to the Americas is Dr. Cyclone Covey (PhD Stanford '49). Since 1953 he has researched and written books on this subject. He and my father were contemporaries but never met. However, Dr. Covey mentioned my father's work in four of his own texts. When I started my own research, I tracked Dr. Covey down and asked difficult but honest questions: "It has been 30 years since my father wrote his book. Has all of this been disproved since?"

Dr. Covey assured me that my father had been right and that in the intervening years much more evidence had come to light. Then he offered to assist were I to continue my father's research. I never could have survived this complicated study without Dr. Covey's guidance and encouragement, which continues to this day. Initially almost everything about this subject was foreign to me, but he has been endlessly patient. He has been my Professor Higgins and I his Eliza Doolittle. At age 89, Dr. Covey graciously and with enthusiasm joined those writing articles for this issue.

Since before the United States was even a nation, in Europe scholars were arguing that Chinese reached the Americas before Columbus. However, century after century they were shouted down. In his 1885 text, *An Inglorious Columbus,* Edward Vining wrote of Philippe Buache, who in Paris in 1753 published a paper stating that in 458 AD, Chinese established a colony on the coast of California. Buache scooped the research of M. de Guignes who in 1761 published, based on a Chinese text, "Investigation of the Navigations of the Chinese to the Coast of America and Some Tribes Situated at the Eastern Extremity of Asia." Perhaps de Guignes had been slow to present his own findings because he knew what had happened to Gallileo only a century earlier when he went against conventional wisdom. At that time and in the centuries following, scholars have arisen with more and more evidence for early Chinese arrival to the Americas—then have been shouted down. As Kermit the Frog said: "It's not easy being green."

Vining's great work is now available as a reprint. His book and de Guignes' research inspired Henriette Mertz in 1953 to write the classic, *Pale Ink,* later published under the title *Gods From the Far East.* Using the verbal descriptions from the Chinese *Shan Hai Jing* and a topographical map, she traced the 2000 BC routes onto maps of the United States, saying that they fit nowhere else on earth. I have been to locations they identify. Too much matches up for it not to be real. The works of Vining and Mertz inspired both my father and Dr. Covey, who lectured widely and wrote *A Critical Reprise of "Aboriginal" American History.* I am aware of several books on different aspects of this topic currently in the pipeline to be published.

My father wrote that it used to be taught in American schools that Chinese had an early presence in the Americas. Though Dr. Covey confirmed this, I had to see it for myself, so I searched antique shops. In *Teachers' and Pupils' Cyclopaedia,* Chicago, 1904, it says, concerning Native Americans, which that text describes as "Indians": "Some ethnologists think they descended from the Mongolian race, while others regard them as a mixture of the Polynesian and Caucasian with the Mongolian. From the tradition of their tribes it is learned that they emigrated from some region, but knew not from whence."

I found that by about 1910, the US history texts suddenly declared that the Indians originated only in the Americas. Of course, DNA now proves the Asian connection. A DNA study in 2010 showed that famed cellist Yo-Yo Ma, whose parents were the first generation to leave China, is genetically related to Eva Longoria of *Desperate Housewives,* who has Native American roots.

My father, Dr. Hendon Harris, Jr., said: "The record of Asia is written into the stones of America and into the bodies of its early people."

Tsinghua University, July 19, 2010, when Chao Chien, S. L. Lee, Charlotte Harris Rees, and Kent Deng spoke there. Left to right are Chao Chien, S. L. Lee, Charlotte Harris Rees, Kong Huai Tsai (descendant of Confucius), Sulia Chan (of New York, who set up the speaking schedule), and Kent Deng.

Everything Under Heaven

Hendon M. Harris, 1973—excerpt from *The Asiatic Fathers of America*

US-China Review, Summer 2011

In August of 1972 I found it necessary to pass through Seoul, Korea. Rising in the morning, I thought I would use my time by visiting antique shops. In a swift reconnaissance mission, I swept through about 25 establishments and was about to return to my hotel... when I entered one last place. I asked the proprietor if he had any books or pictures. He replied: "Would you be interested in a book of old maps?"

When I opened the book, I noticed it contained many ancient cartographic sketches. There was also a very strange-looking map of Japan that must have been made at an extraordinarily early date. And then...I opened the last map...and had to control myself to keep from trembling. It was very old and unusual. "Everything under Heaven" was the title. It was terribly odd. China and Korea took up the center of the world. North of Japan, Asia arched round to Alaska. Down the North American coast it was marked "Fu Sang."

I became weak. I was forced to sit down...

Foreword

We have proof that the Chinese discovered and colonized America thousands of years before the Europeans' arrival.

Approximately 4,200 years ago after a great flood, the Chinese had lost their sense of direction. Therefore, the Emperor found it necessary to send his astronomer Yu to survey the earth, and reestablish the four directions. Yu sent Prince Y across the great eastern ocean, to the land of Fu Sang—literally "land to the east" (the ancient American continents). Prince Y and Yu determined the boundaries of America and other places and afterwards wrote the *Shan Hai Jing.*

The *Shan Hai Jing* (Book of Mountains and Seas) is the world's oldest geography. It tells us of many countries in the ancient Americas. There are reports that Emperor Hwang Ti (2640 BC) probably had sent expeditions or colonies to America. However, we can be certain that Chinese were in the Americas by around 2250 BC.

I have found a map that confirms the 4,200 year old account of the *Shan Hai Jing*. In fact, there are at least thirty similar old round maps in existence, which vindicate and corroborate the report of the *Shan Hai Jing*. These world maps, of ancient origin, are in America, England, France, China, Korea, Japan, and in other countries. The *Shan Hai Jing* told of at least ten countries in America, which are found on my map—the *Harris Fu Sang Map*—and on the maps of similar origin that came from the original *Shan Hai Jing* map.

Proofs that "America" is Fu Sang and the fathers of the Fu Sang people are Chinese are these:

1. The Record of the *Shan Hai Jing*—which describes the people, geography, and the animals.
2. The Record of the ancient Chinese commentaries on the *Shan Hai Jing*. The dates of these commentaries validate the age of the *Shan Hai Jing*.
3. The witness of the American Indians and their traditions and language.
4. The record of those scientists who have studied the blood and physical characteristics of the Chinese "Indian" tribes of North and South America.
5. The ancient round world maps that were previously misunderstood but which we now explain.
6. The Chinese Court Record (Kuen 327) in 501 AD telling of a trip originating in 458 AD to Fu Sang.

The means that the Chinese arrived in the Americas both in 2200 BC and 458 AD was by boat. It is the purpose of this book to give sufficient proof of the realities of these amazing matters. The final result of these revolutionary discoveries will be the greater glory of China, East India, Japan, and Korea and a new respect for and the appreciation of the Indians of North, Central, and South America.

The material of this book is the result of a lifetime of effort. I have been around the world ten times. In India I sought information and in Pakistan and Bangladesh. In Hong Kong and Taiwan I looked for maps and proofs. I went to the British museum and traveled to Berlin to question the Germans.

From the time I was a boy in China until now, I have collected information. In Holland, in Sumatra, in Macao, in Mexico I was searching...searching...searching. At Long Beach, California, and in Seoul, Korea, I received the greatest answers to my quest.

I am writing these lines in Taipei at the house of a Chinese friend. I am no longer young, and old age does not any more seem a far-away time. I am grateful to those who loved and aided me, and to the great God of the heavens, without whose guidance all efforts would have been in vain.

It is my desire that as you consider the lovely long ago morning of Fu Sang, your soul be stirred with a new appreciation of the beauty of life and the innate possibilities of men... that you will hear the music of Man's aspirations, deep in your spirit... and catch a glimpse of the excellent countenance of God.

I hope you will have a more sympathetic awareness of men of other persuasions and be drawn to the True Historian who works all things after His will.

Stone Anchors

US-China Review, Summer 2011

Photo by Dave Rees

Bob Meistrell, founder of Body Glove (wet suits) in Sept. 2010 said he has found about 30 of these when diving off the California coast. Stone cannot be carbon dated. But he was told that judging from the manganese accumulation on them it was estimated that they'd been on the seabed for 3,000 to 4,000 years. The one on the left broke in half as it was hoisted up. Bob said the whole anchor would have weighed a ton. This is the style used by ancient Chinese. Native Americans would not have used such anchors.

US | EUROPE | AFRICA | ASIA | 中文 | **January 12, 2014**

HOME | **CHINA** | **WORLD** | **BUSINESS** | **LIFE** | **CULTURE** | **TRAVEL** | **SPORTS**

OPINION | **REGIONAL** | **MOBILE** ▾ | **NEWSPAPER** ▾

Lifestyle

Fashion	Celebrity	Travel	Food

Health	Video	Photo

Life / News

Mission of discovery, led by ancient maps

By Mike Peters (China Daily)

Updated: 2014-01-12 13:59:21

Charlotte Harris Rees understands that it's hard for many to believe that Chinese could have come to the Americas before Columbus.

She didn't believe her own father.

"For many years I was a skeptic," she says during a recent visit to Beijing. "It wasn't anything personal against my father - it was just that the idea seemed far-fetched and I was too busy with my own life to be bothered."

In 1972, Hendon Harris Jr, a third-generation Baptist missionary living in South Korea, found an ancient Asian world map in an antiques shop, and soon he found others. Stimulated to research what ancients knew about "imaginary" places beyond China, Japan and South Korea, he became entranced by the *Shan Hai Jing* (*Classic of Mountains and Seas*), which has been quoted as folklore in China for centuries. Henriette Mertz, a Chicago attorney, had earlier been similarly intrigued, and in 1953 wrote *Pale Ink*, a book contending that there were 4,000-year-old Chinese trails that could be traced in the Americas.

After the 2003 publication of Gavin Menzies' *1421*, in which the retired submarine navigator makes the case for other Chinese exploration of what we now know as the Americas, Rees and her siblings got curious about the maps their late father had collected and the books he had written - which they'd stashed under a bed and largely forgotten.

Could Dad have been right after all?

125

In her retirement, Rees has been on a 10-year mission of discovery, hoping to find out. Her most recent book, *Did Ancient Chinese Explore America?*, is "my own journey through the Rocky Mountains to find answers", she says.

Sixty years ago, Mertz had relied on historical records to plot the inland journeys she believed early Chinese had made - without making those treks herself. "Taking the *Shang Hai Jing* and modern topographical maps," says Rees, "Mertz drew sketches of four separate journeys that she said the Chinese covered in North America. She claimed that the descriptions fit nowhere else on Earth." Both Mertz and Rees' father believed that such speculative trips would explain oddly specific details about the West coast of "Fu Sang," a land mass on ancient maps where North America sits on modern versions.

From among the four routes that Mertz outlined, Rees and her husband, Dave, chose the route along the Rockies because it was closest to their Virginia home and because "it is probably most like it was long ago", Rees says. "Much of that area is now national parks and nature conservancies. Some of the specified mountains are more than 14,000 feet high, and many wild and dangerous animals live there." Wary of the latter, the couple traveled in winter, specifically because rattlesnakes lie dormant in cold weather.

The Reeses' journey explained some things that had seemed inexplicable. A reference to "bamboo" growing in arid West Texas suddenly became plausible after discussion at a local museum. It could have been river cane, which grew near Chinati Peak - just as Mertz had described. References in *Shan Hai Jing* to gods with human bodies and dragon heads, the author now believes, could be explained by Native American rituals involving frightful masks or the anthropomorphic art - found both in China and the Americas - in which animals take on human characteristics.

"In addition to correctly telling how the rivers flowed, what the mountains looked like, and which minerals were in each location," Rees concludes, her "*Shan Hai Jing* journey" correctly placed a dozen plants and animals endemic North America, and two locations where plants of Chinese origin (white mulberry and ailanthus) are found.

During her recent lecture tour in China, she says, students at Peking University were amazed that Rees' 1,770-kilometer trip might validate the notion that the *Shan Hai Jing* was an actual journey.

But that's just the beginning of the story, Rees says: In those epic old stories, the Chinese explorers didn't stop at Fu Sang. They traveled all over the world.

Endnotes

Endnotes for Chapter 1

1   Gari Ledyard, "Cartography in Korea, Japan, and Vietnam," *History of Cartography*, Vol. 2, Bk. 2, Chicago: The University of Chicago Press, 1995, p. 260

2   "Finding Clues to the Puzzle," *China Daily*, Nov. 10, 2000

3   Charlotte Harris Rees, *Secret Maps of the Ancient World*, Bloomington, IN: Authorhouse, 2008, 2009, pp 35-60

4   Joseph Needham, *Science and Civilisation in China*, Vol. 4, Part 3, 548-549

5   Rees, *Secret Maps of the Ancient World*, p. 90

6   R. A. Barkley, "The Kuroshio Current," http: swfsc.noaa.gov/publications/ CR/1973/7302. PDF

7   Curtis Ebbesmeyer & Eric Scigliano, *Flotsametrics and the Floating World*, New York: Smithsonian Books, 2009, p. 158

8   See Rees, *Secret Maps of the Ancient World*, p. 75-76 or Henriette Mertz, Pale Ink, Chicago: n.p., 1953

Endnotes for Chapter 2

1   John McCrae, "In Flanders Fields," http://www.arlingtoncemetary.net/flanders.htm

2   James Shreeve, "The Greatest Journey," *National Geographic*, March 2006, p. 62

3   "The Territorial Dispute Over Dokdo," http://www.geocities.com/mlovmo/page4.html

4   "Korea to Develop Gas Hydrate Near Dokdo," http://www.dokdonews.net/?p=190

5   *The Timechart History of the World*, Chippenham, England: Barnes and Noble Books, 2004, p. V

6   Temple, Robert, *The Genius of China: 3000 years of Science, Discovery & Invention*, Rochester, Vermont: Inner Traditions, 200, pp 278-281

7   Frank Viviano, "China's Great Armada," *National Geographic*, July 2005, p. 52

8   Richard J. Smith, *Chinese Maps: Images of 'All Under Heaven,'* New York: Oxford University Press, 1996, p. 12

9   China, Japan, and Korea: the Ming, the Qing, Tokugawa, and Chosun," http://afe. easia. columbia.edu/webcourse/key_points/kp_8.htm

10 Smith, p. 54

11 Smith, p. 60

12 Charles O. Hucker, *China to 1850: A Short History,* Stanford, CA: Stanford University Press, 1978

13 "A Timeline of Korean History," http://afe.easia.columbia.edu/timelines/korea_ timeline.htm

14 Hendon Harris, *The Asiatic Fathers of America, Book 2,* Taipei: Wen Ho Printing Co, 1973. pp 184-185

15   Ki-baik Lee, *A New History of Korea,* tr. Edward W. Wagner with Edward J. Shultz, Cambridge, MA: Harvard University Press, 1984, p. 201

16 Ki-baik Lee, p. 180

17 Bae Woo Sung, "Joseon Maps and East Asia," *Korea Journal,* Vol. 48, No. 1, Spring 2008, p. 47

18 Temple, p. 278

19 Sam Lipes and Travis Benard, "Chinese Invention of Paper and Papermaking," http:// wikis. lib.ncsu.edu/index.php/Chinese_Invention_of_Paper_and_Papermaking_-_ Sam_Lipes_and_ Travis_Bernard

20 "The Story of Hanji: Korean Paper that Stands the Test of Time, http://www. visitkorea.or.kr/ enu/CU/CU_EN_8_1_4_1.jsp

21 Temple, p. 127

22 Ki-baik Lee, p. 170

23 "Printing Heritage," http://www.koreanculture.org/06about korea/symbols/11printing heritage.htm.

24 Ki-baik Lee, p. 193

25 Ki-baik Lee, p. 163

26 Ki-baik Lee, pp 210-212

27 Ki-baik Lee, p. 214

28 Ki-baik Lee, p. 214

29 Ki-baik Lee, p. 214

30 Ki-baik Lee, p. 214

31 "China, Japan, and Korea: the Ming, the Qing, Tokugawa, and Chosun," http://afe. easia. columbia.edu/webcourse/key_points/kp_8.htm., p. 4

32 Ki-Baik Lee, p. 268

33   Ki-Baik Lee, pp 334-335

34   "Kohun Period," http://www.mnsu.edu/emuseum/prehistory/japan/japanese_ history.html

35   "China, Japan, and Korea: the Ming, the Qing, Tokugawa, and Chosun," http://afe.easia. columbia.edu/webcourse/key_points/kp_8.htm

36   Daniel Barenblatt, *A Plague Upon Humanity*, New York: Harper Collins, 2004

37   Edward Jewitt Wheeler and Frank Crane, *vol. 67, Current Opinion, 1919, p. 176*

38   Nanba Matsutaro, Muroga Nobuo, Unno Kazutaka, *Old Maps in Japan,* tr. by Patricia Murray, Osaka: Sogensha, Inc., 1973, p. 162

39   https://www.lib.umn.edu/bell/riccimap

Endnotes for Chapter 3

1   Smith, p. 30

2   John M. Hobson, *The Eastern Origins of Western Civilisation*, New York: Cambridge University, Press, 2004, pp 5-6

3   Joseph Needham, *Clerks and Craftsmen in China and the West,* Cambridge: The University Press, 1970, p. 3

4   Needham, *Clerks and Craftsmen in China and the West,* p. 2

5   Leo Bagrow, *History of Cartography,* revised and enlarged by R.A. Skelton, Cambridge, MA: Harvard University Press, 1966, p. 197

6   Smith, p. 25

7   Temple, p. 30

8   Temple, p. 31

9   Bagrow, p. 197

10   Hiroshi Nakamura, *East Asia in Old Maps,* Center for East Asian Cultural Studies, Tokyo: 1964, p. 11

11   Smith, p. 41

12   Smith, p. 59

13   Shannon McCune, *Imago Mundi,* Vol. 4, 1978, p. 112

14   HanYoung-woo, Ahn Hwi-Joon, Bae Woo Sung, tr. Choi Byonghyon, *The Artistry of Early Korean Cartography,* Larkspur, CA: Tamal Vista Publications, 2008, p. 3

15   Han, p. 5

16   Bae, p. 46

17   Han, p. 170

18   Nanba Matsutaro, Muroga Nobuo, Unno Kazutaka, *Old Maps in Japan,* tr. by Patricia Murray, Osaka: Sogensha, Inc., 1973 p. 154

19   Han, p. 103

20   Han, p. 105

21   "Historic Record—Gonyeomangukjeondo" http://sca.seoul.go.kr./english/cultural Asset. jsp?sClssCode=2&sClssCode2=10

22   Han, p. 3

23   Bagrow, p. 204

24   Matsutaro, p. 162

25   "Japanese Maps of the Tokugawa Era—Bankoku sozu" http://angel.library.ubc.ca/cdm4/document.php?CISOROOT=/tokugawa&CISOPTR=481&REC=1

26   Matsutaro, p. 179

27   Matsutaro, p. 160

28   Matsutaro, p. 154

29   Matsutaro, p. 160

Endnotes for Chapter 4

1   Hiroshi Nakamura, "Old Chinese Maps Preserved by Koreans," *Imago Mundi,* Stockholm: 1947, p. 3

2   Ledyard, pp 257-248

3   Oh Sang-Hak, "Circular World Maps of the Joseon Dynasty: Their Characteristics and Worldview," *Korea Journal,* Spring 2008, p. 38

4   Shannon McCune, "The Chonha Do—A Korean World Map," *The Journal of Modern Korean Studies,* Vol. 4, May 1990, p. 3

5   Ledyard, p. 259, footnote 71

6   Lee Chan, *Old Maps of Korea,* Seoul: Korean Library Science Research Institute, 1977 pp 127-128

7   McCune, pp 1-8

8   McCune, p. 5

9   Bagrow, p. 204

10   McCune, p. 3

11   "The J. B. Bernadou Korean Collection 1884-1885," Chang-Su Cho Houchins, Asian Cultural History Program, Smithsonian Institution, 2004, pp 127-128

12   Edward Payson Vining, *An Inglorious Columbus: or Evidence that Hwui Shan and a Party of Buddhist Monks from Afghanistan Discovered America in the Fifth Century, A.D.,* London: D. Appleton and Company, 1885, Elibron Classics reprint, p. 14

13   Vining, p. 13

14   Vining, p. 50

15   H. B. Hulbert, "An Ancient Map of the World," *Bulletin of the American Geographical Society*, Vol. 36, No. 10, 1904, p. 600

16   Yi Ik Seup, "A Map of the World" tr. F. Ohlinger, *The Korean Repository*, Vol. 1, Seoul: Trilingual Press, 1892, p. 337

17   Oh, p. 17

18   Oh, p. 9

19   "Japanese world map," http://usm.maine.edu/maps/oml_map/599?image_id=1

20   Yi, p. 337

21   Smith, pp 24-25

22   Oh, pp 19-20

23   Oh, p. 19

24   Ledyard p. 259

25   Nakamura, *Imago Mundi*, p. 10

26   Anatole Andro, *The 1421 Heresy: An Investigation into the Ming Chinese Maritime Survey of the World*, Bloomington, IN: Authorhouse, 2005, p. 265

27   Harris, Book 2, p. 43

28   McCune, p. 1

29   Hulbert, p. 601

30   Hulbert, p. 602

31   Oh, p. 31

32   Charlotte Harris Rees, ed., *The Asiatic Fathers of America*, Lynchburg, VA: Warwick House, 2006, p. 2

33   Rees, *The Asiatic Fathers of America*, p. 2

34   McCune, p. 5

35   McCune, p. 5

36   Oh, p. 37

37   McCune, p. 1

38   Bagrow, p. 197

39   McCune, p. 3

40   McCune, p. 4

41   Oh, p. 22

42   Oh, p. 27

43   Oh, pp 16-17

44   Lee Chan, p. 223

45   McCune, p. 4

46   Oh, p. 10

47   Oh, p. 16

48   Smith, p. 30

49   Nakamura, p. 10

50   Joseph Needham, "Mathematics and Sciences of the Heavens and Earth," *Science and Civilisation in China,* Vol. 3, New York: Cambridge University Press, 1959, pp 565-567

51   Oh, p. 26

52   Oh, p. 23

53   Oh, p. 25

54   Oh, p. 25

55   Smith, p. 6

56   Ledyard p. 260

57   Ledyard, p. 267

58   Bagrow, p. 204

59   Ledyard, p. 256

60   Ledyard, p. 260

61   Ledyard, p. 262

62   Harris, *The Asiatic Fathers of America,* Book 1, p. 31

63   Oh, p. 11

64   Lee Chan, p. 222

65   Nakamura, p. 22

66   Joseph Needham, "Mathematics and Sciences of the Heavens and the Earth," *Science and Civilisation in China,* Vol. 3, p. 565

67   Needham, *Science and Civilisation in China,* Vol. 3, pp 565-567

68   Ledyard, pp 263-264, quoting Kim Yangson

69   Michael Swift, *Mapping the World,* London: Compendium Publishing Ltd, 2006, p. 54

70   Vincent Virga and the Library of Congress, *Cartographia: Mapping Civilizations,* New York: Little Brown & Co., 2007, p. 62

71   Virga, p. 62

72   "The Great Ocean Conveyor," US Department of Commerce, National Oceanic and Atmospheric Administration, http://oceanservice.noaa.gov/facts/conveyor.html

Endnotes for Chapter 5

1   Smith, p. 49

2   "Matteo Ricci, Li Zhizao, and Zhang Wentao: World Map of 1602" https://www. lib. umn. edu/bell/riccimap

3   Lee Chan, p. 223

4   Smith, p. 43

5   Smith, p. 44

6   Bae, p. 56

7   "News from the Library of Congress," Jan. 12, 2010 http://www.loc.gov/today/ pr/2010/10-002.html

8   "Matteo Ricci, Li Zhizao, and Zhang Wentao: World Map of 1602 http://www.lib. umn.edu/bell/riccimap

9   Rees, *Secret Maps of the Ancient World,* p. 10

10   S. L. Lee, "Zheng He," http://www.asiawind.com/zhenghe/

11   Bae, p. 57

12   Bae, p. 49

13   Deng, Gang, *Chinese Maritime Activities and Socioeconomic Development, c. 2100 B.C.-1900 A.D.,* Westport, CT: Greenwood Press, 1997

14   Bae, p. 50

15   McCune, p. 4

16   Bae, p. 65

17   Bae, p. 66

18   McCune, p. 4

19   Ledyard, pp 269-270

20   Ledyard, p. 271

21   Ledyard, p. 270

22   Kazutaka Unno, "Cartography in Japan," *The History of Cartography:* (Vol. 2, Bk. 2), *Cartography in the Traditional East and Southeast Asian Societies,* Chicago: The University of Chicago Press, 1995, p. 366

23   Unno, p. 367

24   Ledyard, p. 269

25   Smith, p. 2

26   Matsutaro, p. 182

27   Smith, p. 29

28   Ledyard, p. 267

29   Ledyard, p. 267

30   Ki-baik Lee, p. 114

31   Han Young-woo, p. 9

32   Ledyard, p. 306

33   McCune, p. 4

34   McCune, p. 4

35   Han, pp. 160-161

36   Han, p. 161

37   Bagrow, p. 136

38   Raymond H. Ramsay, *No Longer on the Map,* New York: Viking Press, 1972, p. 156

39   Rees, *Secret Maps of the Ancient World, p. 10*

40   Bagrow, p. 199

41   Andro, p. 125

42   Virga, pp. 236-237

Endnotes for Chapter 6

1   Harris, Book 1, p. 267

2   Harris, Book 1, p. 267

3   Bae, pp 46-79

4   Smith, p. 30

5   "Korea to Develop Gas Hydrate Near Dokdo," http://www.dokdonews.net/?p=190

6   Harris, Book 2, pp 189-190

7   "Korean Calligraphy," http://www.britannica.com/EBchecked/media/3333/Chusa- style-written-by-Kim-Chong-Hi-Choson-period

8   "Cao Shu," n.d. Web. 3 Oct. 2011. http://www.wavedancing.net/history/scripts.htm

9   McCune, p. 2

10   Harris, Book 2, p. 190

11   Ledyard, p. 324

Bibliography

Andro, Anatole, The 1421 Heresy: *An Investigation into the Ming Chinese Maritime Survey of the World*, Bloomington, IN: Authorhouse, 2005. Print.

Arnaiz-Villena, A., Parga-Lozano, C., Moreno, E., Areces, C., Rey, D., Gomez-Prieto, P., "The Origin of Amerindians and the Peopling of the Americas According to HLA Genes: Admixture with Asian and Pacific People," *Current Genomics* 11.2 (2010): 103-114. Web. 29 Mar. 2010. <www.ingentaconnect.com/content/ben/cg/2010/00000011/00000002/art00003>.

"A Timeline of Korean History." n.d. Web. 7 Mar. 2011. <http://afe.easia.columbia.edu/timelines/korea_timeline.htm>.

Bae, Woo Sung, "Joseon Maps and East Asia," *Korea Journal* 48.1 (2008): 46-79. Print.

Bagrow, Leo, *History of Cartography,* revised and enlarged by R.A. Skelton, Cambridge: Harvard UP, 1966. Print.

Barenblatt, Daniel, *A Plague Upon Humanity*, New York: Harper Collins, 2004. Print.

Barkley, R. A., "The Kuroshio Current." *Science Journal*, Mar. 1970. n.d. Web. 2 Oct. 2011. <http:swfsc.noaa.gov/publications/CR/1973/7302.PDF>.

"Cao Shu," n.d. Web. 3 Oct. 2011. <http://www.wavedancing.net/history/scripts.htm>.

Chau, Ju-kua, *Chu-fan-chi: His Work on the Chinese and Arab Trade in the Twelfth and Thirteenth Centuries*, tr. Friedrich Hirth and W. W. Rockhill, St. Petersburg: Printing Office of the Imperial Academy of Sciences, 1911, reprint Taipei: Ch'eng-Wen Publishing Company, 1970. Print.

"China, Japan, and Korea: the Ming, the Qing, Tokugawa, and Chosun." n.d. Web. 25 Mar. 2011. <http://afe.easia.columbia.edu/webcourse/key_points/kp_8.htm>.

Covey, Cyclone, *A Critical Reprise of "Aboriginal" American History*, 5th ed. Winston-Salem: Wake Forest U, 2005. Print.

Deng, Gang, *Chinese Maritime Activities and Socioeconomic Development, c. 2100 B.C.-1900 A.D.*, Westport, CT: Greenwood Press, 1997. Print.

Ebbesmeyer, Curtis, and Eric Scigliano, *Flotsametrics and the Floating World: How One Man's Obsession with Runaway Sneakers and Rubber Ducks Revolutionized Ocean Science*, New York: Harper Collins, 2009. Print.

"Finding Clues to the Puzzle," *China Daily*, 10 Nov. 2000. Print.

Han Young-woo, Ahn Hwi-Joon, Bae Woo Sung, tr. by Choi Byonghyon, *The Artistry of Early Korean Cartography*, Larkspur, CA: Tamal Vista Publications, 2008. Print.

Harris, Hendon, *The Asiatic Fathers of America*, two books in one volume, Taipei: Wen Ho Printing Co, 1973. Print.

"Historic Record—Gonyeomangukjeondo." n.d. Web. 25 Mar. 2011. <http:// sca.seoul. go.kr./english/culturalAsset.jsp?sClssCode=2&sClssCode2=10>.

Hobson, John M., *The Eastern Origins of Western Civilisation*, New York: Cambridge UP, 2004. Print.

Hucker, Charles O., *China to 1850: A Short History*, 3rd ed., Stanford, CA: Stanford UP, 1978. Print.

Hulbert, H. B., "An Ancient Map of the World," *Bulletin of the American Geographical Society* 36.10 (1904): 600-605. Print.

"Japanese Maps of the Tokugawa Era-Bankoku sozu." n.d. Web. 25 Mar. 2011. <http://angel.library.ubc.ca/cdm4/document.php?CISOROOT=/ tokugawa&CISOPTR=481&REC=1>.

"Japanese World Map." n.d. Web. 1 Dec. 2010. <http://usm.maine.edu/maps/oml_ map/599?image_id=1>.

"Kohun Period." n.d. Web. 7 Mar. 2011. <http://www.mnsu.edu/emuseum/prehistory/ japan/japanese_history.html>.

"Korean Calligraphy." n.d. Web. 15 Nov. 2010 <http://www.britannica.com/EBchecked/ media/3333/Chusa-style-written-by-Kim-Chong-Hi-Choson-period>.

"Korea to Develop Gas Hydrate Near Dokdo." 25 July 2008. Web. 9 Mar. 2011. <http://www.dokdonews.net/?p=190>.

Ledyard, Gari, "Cartography in Korea, Japan, and Vietnam," *The History of Cartography*: (Vol. 2, Bk. 2), Cartography in the Traditional East and Southeast Asian Societies, Chicago: The U of Chicago P, 1995. Print.

Lee Chan, *Old Maps of Korea*, Seoul: Korean Library Science Research Institute, 1977. Print.

Lee, Ki-baik, *A New History of Korea*, tr. Edward W. Wagner with Edward J. Shultz, Cambridge, MA: Harvard UP, 1984. Print.

Lee, S. L., "Zheng He." 5 July 2010. Web. 2 Oct. 2011. <http://www.asiawind. com/ zhenghe/>.

Lipes, Sam, and Travis Bernard, "Chinese Invention of Paper and Papermaking." n.d. Web. 10 Mar. 2011 <http://wikis.lib.ncsu.edu/index.php/Chinese_Invention_of_Paper_and_ Papermaking_-_>.

Matsutaro, Nanba, Muroga Nobuo, Unno Kazutaka, *Old Maps in Japan*, tr. by Patricia Murray, Osaka: Sogensha, Inc., 1973. Print.

"Matteo Ricci, Li Zhizao, and Zhang Wentao: World Map of 1602." n.d. Web. 10 Mar. 2011. <https://www.lib.umn.edu/bell/riccimap>.

McCrae, John, "In Flanders Fields." n.d. Web. 5 Mar. 2011. <http://www. arlingtoncemetary.net/flanders.htm>.

McCune, Shannon, *Imago Mundi*, 4 (1978): 112. Print.

—. "The Chonha Do—A Korean World Map," *The Journal of Modern Korean Studies* 4 (1990): 1-8. Print.

Mertz, Henriette, *Pale Ink*, Chicago, n.p. 1953. Print.

Nakamura, Hiroshi, *East Asia in Old Maps*, Tokyo: Center for Asian Studies, 1964. Print.

—. "Old Chinese World Maps Preserved by the Koreans," Imago Mundi IV (1947): 1-22. Print.

Needham, Joseph, *Clerks and Craftsmen in China and the West*, Cambridge: The UP, 1970. Print.

—. *Science and Civilisation in China*, 4.3, 548-549, New York: Cambridge UP. Print.

—. "Mathematics and Sciences of the Heavens and Earth," *Science and Civilisation in China* 3, 565-567, New York: Cambridge UP, 1959. Print.

News from the Library of Congress, 12 Jan. 2010. Web. 13 Jan. 2010. <http:// www.loc. gov/today/pr/2010/10-002.html>.

Oh, Sang-Hak, "Circular World Maps of the Joseon Dynasty: Their Characteristics and Worldview," *Korea Journal*, Spring 2008, 9-44. Print.

"Printing Heritage." Web. <http://www.koreanculture.org/06about korea/ symbols/11printing heritage.htm.>.

Ramsay, Raymond H., *No Longer on the Map*, New York: Viking Press, 1972. Print.

Rees, Charlotte Harris, *Secret Maps of the Ancient World*, Bloomington, IN: Authorhouse, 2008. Print.

—. ed., *The Asiatic Fathers of America*, Lynchburg, VA: Warwick House, 2006. Print.

Shreeve, James, "The Greatest Journey," *National Geographic*, March 2006. Print.

Smith, Richard J., *Chinese Maps: Images of 'All Under Heaven,'* New York: Oxford UP, 1996. Print.

Sorenson, John L., and Carl L. Johannessen, *World Trade and Biological Exchanges Before 1492*, New York: iUniverse, Inc., 2009. Print.

Swift, Michael, *Mapping the World*, London: Compendium Publishing Ltd, 2006. Print.

Temple, Robert, *The Genius of China: 3000 years of Science, Discovery & Invention*, 3rd ed., Rochester, Vermont: Inner Traditions, 2007. Print.

"The Great Ocean Conveyor," US Department of Commerce, National Oceanic and Atmospheric Administration. n.d. Web. 2 Oct. 2011. <http://oceanservice. noaa.gov/facts/ conveyor.html>.

"The J. B. Bernadou Korean Collection 1884-1885," Chang-Su Cho Houchins, Asian Cultural History Program, 127-128. Washington: Smithsonian Institution, 2004. Print.

"The Story of Hanji: Korean Paper that Stands the Test of Time." n.d. Web. 2 Oct. 2011. <http://www.visitkorea.or.kr/enu/CU/CU_EN_8_1_4_1.jsp>.

"The Territorial Dispute over Dokdo." n.d. Web. 25 June 2009 <http://www.geocities.com/ mlovmo/page4.html>.

The Timechart History of the World, Chippenham, England: Barnes and Noble Books, 2004. Print.

Unno, Kazutaka, "Cartography in Japan," *The History of Cartography* 2.2, *Cartography in the Traditional East and Southeast Asian Societies*, Chicago: The U of Chicago P, 1995. Print.

Vining, Edward Payson, *An Inglorious Columbus: or Evidence that Hwui Shan and a Party of Buddhist Monks from Afghanistan Discovered America in the Fifth Century, A.D.*, London: D. Appleton and Company, 1885, Elibron Classics reprint. Print.

Virga, Vincent, and the Library of Congress, *Cartographia Mapping Civilizations*, New York: Little Brown & Co, 2007. Print.

Viviano, Frank, "China's Great Armada," *National Geographic*, July 2005. Print.

Wheeler, Edward Jewitt and Frank Crane, vol. 67, *Current Opinion*, 1919. Print.

Yi, Ik Seup, "A Map of the World" tr. F. Ohlinger, *The Korean Repository* 1, Seoul: Trilingual Press, 1892, reprint New York: Paragon Book Reprint Corp, 1964. Print.

About The Author

Charlotte Harris Rees has appeared on television and National Public Radio in the United States and Canada and in numerous international news articles about her family's map collection and her research concerning the very early arrival of Chinese to America.

She has given many presentations including at the Library of Congress (Washington, DC); The National Library of China (Beijing); Stanford University; the University of London; Tsinghua University (Beijing); University of British Columbia; Zheng He Symposium (Melaka, Malaysia); Switzerland; the University of Maryland; City University of New York; Seton Hall University; the Chinese Historical Society (Los Angeles); and the Royal Geographical Society (London and Hong Kong).

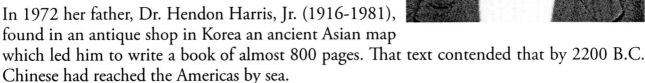

In 1972 her father, Dr. Hendon Harris, Jr. (1916-1981), found in an antique shop in Korea an ancient Asian map which led him to write a book of almost 800 pages. That text contended that by 2200 B.C. Chinese had reached the Americas by sea.

Since early 2003, Rees, an independent researcher, a retired federal employee, and an honors graduate of Columbia International University, has diligently studied the possibility of very early arrival of Chinese to America. Her mentor, Dr. Cyclone Covey, has researched this China/America connection for 60 years.

In 2003 Rees and her brother took the *Harris Map Collection* to the Library of Congress where it remained for three years while being studied. In 2006 she published an abridged version of her father's, *The Asiatic Fathers of America: Chinese Discovery and Colonization of Ancient America*. Her *Secret Maps of the Ancient World* came out in 2008. In late 2011 she released the first edition of *Chinese Sailed to America Before Columbus: More Secrets from the Dr. Hendon M. Harris, Jr. Map Collection*. In 2013 she published *Did Ancient Chinese Explore America? My Journey Through the Rocky Mountains to Find Answers*. Her books are listed by World Confederation of Institutes and Libraries for Chinese Overseas Studies and are endorsed by Dr. Hwa-Wei Lee, retired Chief of the Asian Division of the Library of Congress.

Her father, Dr. Harris, a third generation Baptist missionary, was born in Kaifeng, China. As a child Rees lived for four years in Taiwan then later for a year in Hong Kong. In recent years she has taken several trips to China. Her home is in Virginia.

Additional Resources

Did Ancient Chinese Explore America? My Journey Through the Rocky Mountains to Find Answers tests the hypothesis that ancient Chinese geographical descriptions of the "Eastern Mountains" actually referenced locations in North America. In this travelogue Rees candidly shares her initial doubts then her search and discoveries as she follows an 1100 mile trek through the Rocky Mountains. She weaves together history, subtle humor, academic studies, and many photographs to tell a compelling story.

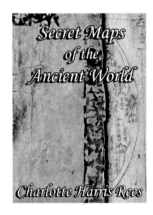

Secret Maps of the Ancient World brings together an abundance of worldwide academic evidence that Asians reached the Americas at very early dates. It also compares peoples on both sides of the Pacific, discusses DNA, and relates how Asians could have traveled to the Americas by sea. The capstone of the book is an ancient Asian map shown in museums around the world, which until recently was thought to be part imaginary. The thesis of the book is that secrets on those maps were hidden for years in plain sight.

The Asiatic Fathers of America: Chinese Discovery and Colonization of Ancient America emphasizes the many early Chinese writings that discussed Fu Sang, a beautiful land to the East of China. However, over thousands of years most forgot where Fu Sang was. Then in 1972 Dr. Hendon Harris, Jr. (Charlotte Harris Rees's father) discovered an antique Asian map which shows Fu Sang on the American coastline. Harris discusses early Chinese literary descriptions of the Grand Canyon and other geographical features of North America. He compares human characteristics. This book is Charlotte's abridgment and edit of her father's original tome of almost 800 pages.

Dr. Hendon M. Harris, Jr. Map Collection on CD contains over 100 high definition photos showing all the maps in the Harris collection – some both front and back. Available only through www.AsiaticFathers.com

www.AsiaticFathers.com

CPSIA information can be obtained at www.ICGtesting.com
Printed in the USA
BVOW02s1319030614

355205BV00010B/85/P